THE RELIGION RACKET
Norman H. Wells

The Religion Racket
by Norman H. Wells

Reprinted by permission of James H. Dearmore and
Gospel Web of Garland, Texas. *www.gospelweb.net*

Current edition published in 2015
by Victory Baptist Press
Milton, Florida — USA

13: 978-0-9792562-1-9
10: 0-9792562-1-6

Cover design by Aaron Ebert.
Layout by Sarah Berg and Trinity Lorimer.

CONTENTS

FOREWORD

I have been the pastor of a thriving Baptist church for more than 18 years. It is from this vantage point that I have viewed religion.

This book is an attempt to record some of these observations. I have written about general conditions and am very much aware of the fine exceptions to what I have written that exist in religion.

My life has been dedicated to a proclamation of religious truth. The desire of my life, and the purpose of this book, is to remove some of the debris that covers this truth.

I have tried to use every weapon available to accomplish my purpose. The battering ram of ridicule and the rapier of satire are used, along with the gentleness of a quiet laugh at ourselves.

The words in this book had to be spoken. It could be wished that a more eloquent voice had been raised, but since none has, I have done what I could.

Norman H. Wells
Author

Chapter 1
Jesus Christ Versus Religion

"Ye serpents, ye generation of vipers, how can ye escape the damnation of hell?" It was shots like this that Jesus fired as He began attacking the entrenched position of the organized, established religion of His day. The religious atmosphere began to crackle with the intensity of the charges He leveled. These were not powder-puff taps, but sledgehammer blows. When Jesus engaged the religionists in combat, it was not just a routine, minor skirmish between competing religious scholars over some minor theological question, but was a declaration of all-out war, a fight to the finish. There was no mistaking His language nor to whom it was directed. It was not aimed at the drunk in the gutter nor the harlot on the corner, but at the respected, refined religionists quarreling over the uppermost rooms in their ornate houses of worship. This was not language that was refined with subtleties and niceties until it lost all force. This was a punch in the nose, and there was no mistaking the intent because it rocked the religionists right down to their broad phylacteries.

It became immediately obvious that Christ saw no hope in reclamation or revitalization of the existing religious establishment. He looked upon it as a failure and a hindrance and set about to plow it under in order to plant a new crop. Slugging it out in head-to-head conflict with the religionists is a part of the ministry of Christ that receives little attention, yet the blow-by-blow account of this struggle runs through all four Gospels. Jesus Christ versus religion!

The battle lines were drawn and Jesus quickly identified the enemy. The religionists would march up to Jesus in all their regal splendor, and He would shoot them down by declaring, "Ye are of your father the devil" (John 8:44). They reeled back in utter disarray as He charged that theirs was "the greater damnation" (Matt. 23:14). The population listened in amazement, and in the heart of some there began to grow the thrill of recognizing that here was one, openly and bravely, voicing that which they had timidly and secretly, long felt to be true. The furor increased and there was no room left for compromise as Jesus cried out that the religionists were the children of hell who were not going to enter the kingdom of heaven! He said they opposed God and persecuted His spokesmen. This was a showdown, and in this conflict there would have to emerge a victor and a loser; there would be no in-between, no compromise.

The long robes of the religious leaders must have trembled as they shook in rage before the onslaught of Christ as He charged, "[Y]e shut up the kingdom of heaven against men" (Matt. 23:13). This was a body blow. Not only, Christ declared, were these religious leaders not entering into the kingdom of heaven, but also they were keeping others from entering. Not only did Jesus describe them as children of hell, but said they were guilty of enticing those they were leading into the same condition. To be accused of cutthroat murder would have been mild in comparison to this charge.

In all probability, the righteousness of the religious establishment had never been questioned. No one would dare! Their piety and holiness were known and spoken of far and wide. A great part of their activities dealt with virtue and cleanliness. Christ acknowledged these well-known traits when He said, "[Y]e also outwardly appear righteous unto men," but shot it down when He added, "but within ye are full of hypocrisy and iniquity" (Matt. 23:28). Hypocrisy! How this charge must have cut. Christ said they were only concerned about cleaning the outside of the cup while "within they [were] full of extortion and excess" (Matt. 23:25).

Hypocrisy! Over and over, this charge was hurled. As the religious leaders piously stood in the streets making long prayers, Jesus said it was all a pretense and He warned that the religionists "say, and do not" (Matt. 23:3).

To demonstrate their love for the Scriptures, the religionists would strap portions of the Scriptures around their heads and arms. Christ looked at this practice and declared the only reason they had for doing this was "to be seen of men" (Matt. 23:5). Pride! Making a show of their religion! Christ exposed this pride when He said they "love the uppermost rooms at feasts, and the chief seats in the synagogues" (Matt. 23:6). He added that they loved to hear themselves addressed by fancy religious titles. Their chief concern in their religion was to impress other men.

Jesus recognized that all reality in religion had been buried under the multiplied minute precepts and distinctions of the pompous religionists. The inner experience had been sacrificed to the outward appearance. The spirit had been smothered by hundreds of interpretations of the letter, and this had finally led to an acceptance of error in preference to the truth. Jesus said the religionists had "taken away the key of knowledge" (Luke 11:52) and were "teaching for doctrines the commandments of men" (Matt. 15:9). They were "blind leaders of the blind" (Matt. 15:14).

After recovering from the first stunning impact of this onslaught, the religionists counterattacked with vigor. "He hath a devil" (John 10:20), they cried. They accused Him of blasphemy and held councils how they might entangle Him in His talk and discredit Him before the people. They made repeated attempts to destroy Him and finally succeeded as they delivered Him up to be executed.

One cannot read the Gospels without being aware of this conflict between Christ and religion. He deliberately exposed the sham, deceit, hypocrisy, pride, error, and failure of the established religion and warned against its deadly, smothering effect. He knew it had to be swept away before the reality of the truth that He brought could be felt.

In our generation, the worship and service of the God of the Bible again finds itself encrusted with the same kind of accumulation, and the desperate need is to allow the words of Christ to expose this condition and destroy it so that the truth and reality of religion might again shine forth. Religion today bears the same characteristics that Jesus so vigorously condemned. The four or five sects that represented the worship of the living God in the time of Christ have been replaced by the dozens of different denominations and cults of today, but the same deadly diseases still plague them: deceit, sham, hypocrisy, pride, error, and failure. One doesn't have to be an authority on religion or make an in-depth study of each of these denominations to arrive at these conclusions. All one has to do is look at the product of these denominations; that is, Christianity as it is in America today.

Religion in the United States today is a failure, in the same manner as religion during the time of Christ's earthly ministry. There is nothing, absolutely nothing, as worthless as a religion that does not work. To be weighted down with a worthless religion is a constant frustration. One of the truly amazing things is why a people who will not tolerate failure anywhere else will so meekly accept it in religion. Practically every place where religion is supposed to exert an influence, it is being defeated. It is failing to meet the spiritual needs of the individual. Instead of the love, joy, and peace that religion should impart, we have a continual increase in tension, anxiety, and fear. Real religion is a deterrent to crime, yet we find ourselves caught up in a constant increase of crime and lawlessness. Disregard for law and order has become an accepted way of life, and today's religion is having little or no effect. The moral strength of this country is in a steady decline. Everywhere, materialistic values are being substituted for spiritual ones. Religion is failing, while immorality is flourishing, and juvenile delinquency is on the rise. The moral standards that religion has set are flouted and ridiculed. Pornography and smut are accepted and preferred in our literature, movies, and stage shows, and religion seems to make no impact. Drunkenness continues to be one of our greatest problems and increases year after year. Again, religion has failed. A nation founded upon deep religious convictions is now systematically purging itself of this identity. In every aspect of life where religion is a factor, it is failing.

The Religion Racket

Is it possible for anyone today to even briefly entertain the thought that if Christ walked our streets on any Sunday morning, looked at the hundreds of fine church buildings, heard the organs and singing, listened to the sermons, and observed the people, that He would again cry out, "Ye serpents, ye generation of vipers, how can ye escape the damnation of hell?" In all probability, no one would give this kind of thinking much, if any, consideration. It is too easy to prove that religion is a "success." Religion has more money, more people, more prestige, more buildings, more schools, more hospitals, and more missionaries: just about more of everything than at any time in all history. Why, just about everyone belongs to some church: the government leaders, the bankers, the doctors, the lawyers, the movie stars, the leading sports figures, et cetera. How much more religious can you get? It is almost impossible for today's religionist to even for a moment think that the language of Christ could apply to today's religion as well as when the words were first spoken. It was surely our generation that Jesus had in mind when He said, "Because thou sayest, I am rich, and increased with goods, and have need of nothing; and knowest not that thou art wretched, and miserable, and poor, and blind, and naked" (Rev. 3:17). Any honest appraisal of religion today would reveal that spiritually it is wretched, miserable, poor, blind, and naked, but religion will not look. It is too busy impressing everyone with facts and figures that prove success. Why is it so difficult to be honest about religion?

In every aspect of human life where religion is a factor, it is failing. This failure is obvious, but the amazing thing is that no one seems to be willing to acknowledge it is happening. Most religion goes right on making the colossal pretense that all is well and that religion is marching victoriously onward and upward. This refusal to admit failure and the insistence upon keeping up the pretense of success has produced a religion that is a deliberate deception. Too often, religion has chosen to deny its obvious failure and to give itself to a promotion or a pretense of success.

Not only is today's religion failing, but it is also looked upon as a fake. It no longer is fulfilling its purpose for existence, but continues to pretend that it does. Deliberate deception with the design of securing unfair advantage or allegiance is fraud. Most of religion today would come under this indictment. It operates under false pretenses. It promises but does not deliver. It blatantly demands respect for its deceits and solicits support for its fraudulent designs. This is a racket: a religion racket!

The amazing thing is that so many recognize that most of today's religion is a fraud and yet approvingly accept it as such. Our inherited respect and reverence forbid us to unmask this religion racket. In honesty, we cannot accept it, and our spiritual need won't let us reject it. To be at least half safe we give it token toleration. To a great number, the deliberate deceptions and fraudulent claims of much of today's religion have become so obvious that they look upon it as a ridiculous farce. And it is!

The tragedy is that real religion is buried under the maze of contradicting claims, tired traditions, and deliberate deceits of this racket in religion. It has cloaked itself in superficial sanctity and hides from honest appraisal. It is time to bring today's religion out into the light of a full investigation of its reality, not its pretense.

The Religion Racket

Reliable religion has to do with man's relationship to his God and to his fellow man. It will saturate his entire being and bring about conformity of his heart and life to his religious beliefs. The effect of a man's religion will reveal itself in every aspect of his life. It will express itself in dedicated worship, sacrificial service, and holy, honorable living. It determines our morals and eternal destiny. Religion has to do with the spiritual, the supernatural, and the eternal. Religion, by its very nature, must be accepted as of supreme importance or be utterly rejected. Here, above all else, we should be true and genuine. There should be a profound sacredness that would penetrate and influence our entire existence.

Sacred and spiritual things should demand solemn, serious, penetrating consideration. Our worship should express a reverence bathed in respect and esteem. Our purpose is to exalt and to magnify in humble adoration. In religion, man is to find the fulfillment of his purpose for existence. Its fruitage is the realization of the peace, joy, and love that man must have.

Contrast real religion with the current crop of counterfeits, and we will find nothing more than shallow substitutes. Are we ready for this? Are we willing to refuse the substitute and to demand the real thing? Are we ready to discard our sacred shams and pompous pretenses? Are we ready to be honest about religion?

If all this sounds vaguely familiar to you, it might be because it has all been said before. One of the prophets wrote, "[T]his people draw near me with their mouth, and with their lips do honour me, but have removed their heart far from me" (Isa. 29:13). Christ described the religionists of His day as hypocrites that "say and do not." He also said, "All their works they do to be seen of men," and they "for a pretense make long prayers." Christ denounced the pretense in His day in no uncertain terms. He said, "Even so ye also outwardly appear righteous unto men, but within ye are full of hypocrisy and iniquity" (Matt. 23:28). When He looked at their worship service, He said, "In vain do they worship me." It was said of churchgoers, "They profess that they know God; but in works they deny him" (Titus 1:16).

This condition had to be exposed and destroyed before Christianity could be born. It will again have to be exposed and destroyed if Christianity is to be reborn in our generation.

Chapter 2
Habitual Hypocrisy

In religion, we have persistently practiced pretense so long that it has become a way of life: habitual hypocrisy.

In matters of religion, the average individual recognizes the weakness of his spiritual situation. He knows what he should be, but feels it is unobtainable. He settles for an in-between land of make-believe and in some way produces a pretense of religion. This has become standard practice and is the accepted thing. Habitual hypocrisy! This habitual hypocrisy produces some strange goings-on.

A religious individual will enjoy the worship services of his religion. This is where he feasts upon the wonderful blessings provided by his religion. He hungers for these blessings and finds in them his chief delight and satisfaction. He responds as a thirsty man to a cool spring of water, as a lonely man to the laughter of friends. This joy is not found, however, in the average churchgoer of today. Rather than a happy response to the call to worship, there is generally a hostile reluctance. The average church is trying to provide a religious diet for people who have no religious appetite and, thus, finds itself in the ridiculous position of having to pretend the folks whom it is trying to force to partake are hungry for religion. The labor of religion degenerates into coaxing and pleading for people to look as though they enjoy what they really detest. This results in the average worshipper having to pretend to enjoy what he finds extremely boring and to pretend to dislike what he finds alluring. He is somewhat like the dinner guest who finds that the main dish is a food that he absolutely dislikes but finds it necessary to choke it down while pretending that it is delicious.

Habitual hypocrisy produces some of the strangest excuses for not attending the services of worship. Very few people like to go to work, yet nearly everyone will get to work promptly five or six days a week. Everyone is supposed to enjoy going to church one day a week, yet a great percentage find it impossible to get up in time. Supposedly, it is possible to consistently get up and do what is disliked but impossible to get up and do what is liked.

A family has clothes to wear everywhere else but to church.

A mother sends her child off to school five days a week in rain, sleet, and snow, but will only bring the same child to Sunday school and church if the weather is perfect and a doctor has given him a clean bill of health the day before. We provide a child with 30 hours a week in public school and one hour a week in spiritual training. We tell him that spiritual things are the most important and are amazed when he doesn't believe it. When the child is an infant, he is too young to bring to church, and as a toddler, he is kept home the majority of time to protect him from disease. When he is older, he won't behave and is again kept home. When he becomes a teenager, he refuses to go and we wonder why.

A large family has a built-in excuse. They do not attend church unless all of the family can come. In such a large family, something is always wrong with at least one of them so they very seldom attend.

Our habitual hypocrisy makes us say that our worship and service are the first things in our life, while in reality we give priority to almost everything else.

Habitual hypocrisy naturally produces perpetual liars. The greater percentage of those who continually are absent from the services of the church will promise faithfully to be present the next Sunday even though they have no real intention of doing so. Everybody accepts this as a routine part of the game. Yes, habitual hypocrisy produces some strange goings-on.

Religion is supposed to be characterized by brotherly love. In reality, the average church is a place of fretful feuding and frequent fighting. It is a place where folks seem to be forever fussing. A large percentage of today's churches were started by groups who got licked in a church fight and had to move out. It seems people are harder to get along with in church than anywhere else. If a man were as contentious at his place of employment as he is in church he'd be fired in a week.

In the average church, the battle lines are drawn and the fight is on. Warring factions seek favorable positions and constantly seek to add to their number. Super-sensitive saints walk around with their feelings sticking out like a radar's antenna, constantly challenging anyone to make contact. These folks make a career of contention.

Habitual hypocrisy produces a brotherly love that expresses itself in contentious cliques, fighting factions, and petty partisanism. For a demonstration, attend the business meeting of a local church.

The average pastor has to care for his congregation in the manner of a nursery worker with a roomful of babies with diaper rash. It can be said that the quarreling and fussing of the church is like that of brothers and sisters in a large family. It is loud and contentious, but underneath it all is love. If this is true, why try to pretend the situation doesn't exist?

Yes, habitual hypocrisy does produce some strange goings-on. We say we go to church to worship. Why we really go is an entirely different thing. Instead of a "gospel center," the average church has become a "gossip center." It is where one goes to pick up and pass on the latest bit of gossip. The battle of the backbiters! One thing about these people, they are regular in attendance. To be absent is to become the target of the tales that will be told.

Then there is the one who loves to have the preeminence. He has found that the church is about the only place where he's paid any attention. His wife won't let him talk at home and his boss won't listen at work, but in the church, he's somebody important. He finds that everything he does gets attention and acclaim. He thrives on this until he finally expects a standing ovation every time he shows up. It is a common thing for these people to move from one small church to another. They like to be a big voice in a little choir. They usually change churches about the second time they do something that is not given wide acclaim and pulpit recognition.

Going to church is such a good thing. It gives one a chance to parade his piety and ventilate his virtue. How wonderful to be good...one hour a week. One hour of holiness is about all the average churchgoer can stand in one week.

Fear and guilt are large factors in why people go to church. It is not generally known what is feared or why there is guilt, but it is known these fears and guilt become greater when one does not attend church, so we attend. Then again, where can you get all dressed up and go that costs so little? And the entertainment is getting better!

Habitual hypocrisy does produce some strange goings-on. Think of the money and effort the average church will put forth to secure the services of a highly trained "doctor of divinity" to whom they are not going to listen. They knowingly pay for what they are going to use. The sermon has to be good, even if they're not. They pay the doctor and then won't accept the remedy. There is seemingly no relationship between the lofty phrases of Sunday morning and the reality of life on Monday morning. The unreality of religion in the life of those inside the church makes it easy for those on the outside to turn away in unbelief.

Let us throw away the pretense and hypocrisy. If our religion is what we say, let's embrace it wholeheartedly. If it is not, let us in all honesty reject it equally and wholeheartedly.

Chapter 3
Hallelujah Hucksters

Since the average churchgoer is living in pretense and has no appetite for real religion, it has been necessary to make some adjustments. Instead of dedicated worship and sacrificial service, we have what might be called ecclesiastical entertainment. Our religious services are dedicated to the amusement of the assembled adherents.

Today's sophisticated churchgoer can shop through the religious page of his Saturday paper and find out what will be playing in the various churches on Sunday. It will be noticed that sometimes it is difficult to distinguish between the religious page and the amusement page. On the religious page it can be noted what gospel celebrities are in town and where they are appearing. A church is very fortunate to have a guest appearance by a gospel celebrity. These celebrities usually appear in exchange for the privilege of plugging their latest record, books, or religious trinkets. Broken-down entertainers who couldn't make it in show business have found that by giving their act a religious veneer, they have a ready market in the churches. Everything from magicians to broncobusters is on the church circuit. The pay isn't good but it is getting better. Preachers have retaliated by entering the entertainment field with religious acts.

The Religion Racket

Every successful religious show must have a "name" attraction. These stars must be well traveled, well known, and have good reviews. These reviews are important because they reveal what kind of crowds the star has attracted, how many converts he has had, how much money he can raise, et cetera. A gospel celebrity is very jealous about his reviews because they are his bread and butter. These reviews are important, and since they are generally written by the performer himself, there develops a slight tendency to exaggerate. These reviews will sometimes speak of crowds of several thousand attending services in an auditorium with less than eight hundred seats! One review kept stating that the auditorium was always comfortably full whenever the star gave a performance. This was very impressive until someone found out that by "comfortably" full he meant everyone had room enough to lie down.

Reading all these reviews together would convince anyone that all of America was converted last week. Twice! To attend one of these meetings after reading the reviews telling of the tremendous crowds and glorious services can be a little disappointing. One man, after reading these great reviews, found that every time he attended, the services were dull and the crowd was small. He finally concluded he must be some kind of Jonah, and it would be better for everyone if he didn't attend. Sometimes when a churchgoer reads the reviews of meetings he has attended, he is tempted to wonder where he was when all that happened.

The big demand today is for good singing groups. Family singing groups are particularly popular. These groups have successfully modernized the old-time religion. They keep up

with the latest trends, styles, and fashions of the entertainment world and add just enough religious flavor to get by.
These groups have the same hairstyles, dress, music, and manners of any other rock and roll group, but they know how to
sprinkle their songs with choice, standard, religious phrases.

Today's successful religious services have become a carefully
produced theatrical production for the delight of the church
audience. This entertainment might range from operatic
arias to country and western hoedowns, from Shakespeare
to cheap vaudeville acts, but entertainment it is: nothing
more. Audience participation shows are also popular. Fun
and games for everyone. Prizes galore and everyone has a
chance to win. Everybody sing. It's not raining on the inside.
Game shows come in for a big play. Contests are always big.
Participation and competition are tried and proven winners.

The Sunday morning floor show will regularly feature the
same basic format: a good musical program, guest celebrities, a stand-up comic, and a good master of ceremonies who
must also excel in extracting money. A news commentator
with religious overtones is always good. All this must run
smoothly and fit neatly into the allotted time.

This association of religious truth with mere entertainment
has so cheapened the truth, that one takes it no more seriously than he does the patter of a nightclub comic. If what we
want is entertainment, let's be honest enough to call it that,
and quit trying to disguise it as religion.

In general, religion has become a big business with hallelujah hucksters peddling packaged piety and bargain blessings.
Our ministers have become merchants of morality who spend

their time promoting instead of preaching. The latest selling methods are employed, and religion finds itself commercialized and dispensed in convenient, easy-to-take capsules.

Today's religion is a highly competitive business. In order to sell his particular brand, the preacher must meet the demands of the public better than his competition. His program must be popular, his preaching painless, and there must be a constant presentation of coming attractions that will entice the people to return. He must constantly awaken the congregation with parties, pageants, and pep meetings. These sanctuary slumberers become hypodermic saints living on shots of religious excitement. Religion has become a product that is peddled from our pulpits. All this has produced an almost carnival atmosphere in some of our churches. Competitive contests are held with prizes for those who can round up the largest number of reluctant sinners on any special day. Spiritual "specials" are common. Celebrity guests with gospel glamour. Special speakers, ex-movie stars, and ex-crooks are the "come-ons" that feature "giveaways." Balloons for the kids, ballpoint pens for the adults, and for the grand prize winner, a beautiful, red-letter Bible autographed by the pastor.

All the gimmicks and gadgets of modern merchandising and advertising are brought over into our religious business. No Sunday can be just a plain Sunday, a day of worship. It has to be a "special day." Never an ordinary Sunday, but 52 special days a year is the rule.

A Baptist gentleman who was not attending church was visited by the local pastor who invited him to the church services on the next Sunday. The response was, "Why? What's going on?"

All this has produced religion with the spirituality of a vaude-ville act playing in a shopping center. It evolves through various stages of polish and sophistication until it arrives at the dignity and decorum of a broker's office. The only thing that changes is the method of merchandising and advertising. Hard sell or soft sell? Shout forth the sales pitch like a side-walk vendor or give it scholarly over a mahogany desk. If the hallelujah huckster is successful, he becomes an evangelical executive in a gray flannel suit; some start out that way.

Most ministers fit somewhere between the hollering, halle-lujah huckster and the polite, polished, pulpit politician. The hallelujah huckster comes on with the gusto of a used car salesman giving a commercial on television, while the pulpit politician uses the approach of the local, friendly under-taker trying to convince the bereaved family to buy a higher priced casket.

The pulpit politician considers himself a divine diplomat. He is the poor man's philosopher. He is a master at arranging words to have no meaning. He can always give a lengthy dis-cussion of the good and bad of both sides of any question but never commits himself to either. He packages his product with rhetorical religious expressions and masks it in mystery. The consumer is never sure of what he has bought or if it has any use. He buys it to make sure he has it just in case a need arises.

Another type of hallelujah huckster that seems to meet with a great deal of success is what might be called a clerical comedian. His method is simply to deliver a brief, humorous, monologue once or twice a week in the manner of the night-club stand-up comic. He gets everybody in a good humor

21

and hopes the audience will buy. The clerical comedian takes a very small amount of truth and mixes it with a large amount of humor in order to make it palatable to the consumer.

Then there is the preacher who is nothing more than a master of ceremonies. His main task is simply to introduce the different acts that have been assembled for the entertainment of his congregation. He presents the Gospel in little one-minute commercials given between the acts.

In our pulpits, we also have the medicine man. He conducts services in the manner of the old-time medicine shows. Come one, come all, and bring your aches and pains, stresses, and strains. The miracle man will cure them all.

Among the clergy are those who could only be described as glamour boys, real matinee idols. They keep up with the latest fashions in men's clothing and their cologne is always the latest scent. Their hair is styled, their fingernails glisten, and their cuff links flash. They are real dolls. These glamour boy preachers present themselves as the hero of every story they tell and every illustration they use reveals their magnificence. They generally gather a following of what might be described as "preacher worshippers." They transfer the religious loyalties of the people to themselves.

Hallelujah hucksters. Merchants of morality. Promoters. Evangelical executives. Pulpit politicians. Divine diplomats. Clerical comedians. Masters of ceremonies. Medicine men. Spiritual specialists. Glamour boys. Who needs them?

We need to turn from vague vanities and listen for a victorious voice from God. We need preachers who will stand and proclaim what God has said without fear or favor. We need preachers who care not about comfortable careers but about the urgency of conveying communications from God to man. We need preachers, not pitchmen! Pastors, not peddlers!

Chapter 4
United We Fall

Religion has the arrogant audacity to look the world square in the eye and make the preposterous proclamation that all the hundreds of competing churches with their bigoted beliefs, contradicting creeds, and diverse doctrines are really one religion.

All religions are obligated to accept what they believe and teach to be truth. When the "truth" of one church contradicts the "truth" of another church, one thing becomes painfully obvious. They might both be wrong, but they can't both be right. Many make the claim of being the "true" church. This naturally means that all that differ have to be accepted as false.

Practically every church has a creed, which gives a summary of their religious beliefs and doctrines. Using all of these creeds, one can find a denial of every positive truth that is proclaimed in any of the creeds. Anything that one church believes is denied by another.

An honest outsider making inquiry of the many different churches would not only conclude that there were many different religions, but also that there were many different gods.

Religion in our day ranges from the snake-handling preacher performing his miracles in a downtown storefront, to the cardinal observing the complications of a High Mass in some ornate cathedral. And we are supposed to believe that they are all one religion.

A family will move and have to change churches. They will generally start attending the church that is closest to their new home. Their new church may be entirely different in creed and practice, but they are still to believe that they are in the same religion. A family of 10 could each attend a different church. These 10 churches could be different and contradicting, yet this family would be expected to believe they were all in the same religion.

Church "A" will proclaim that if you believe what they say, you are heaven-bound, but church "B" will declare that if you believe what church "A" teaches, you are hell-bound. This, it must be said, is quite a difference! In this one religion, you can have a God that is dead or one that is living.

Baptism can mean anything from being dipped three times under water to having three drops sprinkled on your head. To some, baptism is a way to heaven, while others say it isn't even necessary to be baptized. Babies are baptized by some, while others denounce this as heresy.

The Bible can be either the infallible, inerrant Word of God or a mere collection of myths, traditions, and wise sayings of men. God created this world by speaking it into existence six thousand years ago, or He merely sat back and watched it evolve over several million years.

Some of the religions ignore eternal things and concentrate on the betterment of man in this life, while others, quite the opposite, ignore this world and spend their time preparing for the next.

To be saved or not to be saved, that is the question. Salvation is emphasized by some as the most important thing in man's existence, while others ignore it entirely. One church declares that an eternal hell of literal fire and brimstone awaits the unrepentant sinner, while another yawns and declares hell doesn't exist. One religion says man is eternal and immortal, and another says he is not. Quite a difference!

What about man? Some say that he is bad and getting worse, while others say he is good and getting better. We can hear that this world is reeling toward fiery destruction, or it is spiraling upward to utopia.

Ask a question and all these churches come up with different answers. That is bad enough, but then for religion to expect us to believe that all these different answers are right and true is downright ridiculous. Suppose an arithmetic teacher gave a class of 10 pupils one problem, got from them 10 different answers, and then would announce they were all correct. That is foolishness.

Some people see the foolishness of this and try to remedy it with something even more foolish. These people will disavow any relationship with any established denomination and will call themselves interdenominational. This can mean just about anything, but it is presented as a religion acceptable to people of all denominations. Now this would take some doing! All the so-called "truths" of the various denominations that contradict and deny each other are all accepted.

The Religion Racket

Does that sound foolish and confusing? There's more. There are those who are un-denominational. This has to mean they are not of any denomination. People of all faiths and religious beliefs are welcome to be members of this un-denominationalism. This has got to produce a big nothing!

The greatest emphasis in religion today is that given to the ecumenical movement. This is the effort to bring all the different churches, denominations, and religions together with the idea of eventually becoming one church. This is a real paradox! These same people will have us believe that we are already one church, and yet they spend a lot of time and money trying to establish what they say already exists!

For the ecumenical movement to be successful, it becomes necessary for each participating religion to soften, tone down, and eventually get rid of its distinctive doctrines that are not in harmony with all the other participating religions. Anything that is believed by one and not by another must eventually be eliminated. Since everything that anyone believes is denied by another, this does eventually produce unity: unity in unbelief. This is where the ecumenical epidemic will finally lead.

Why can't we turn from this feeble folly of pretense and face the situation? We need to acknowledge that what we have is a host of different religions. We must accept that not all of them can be right and that each of us has the task of finding the truth in this maze of contradiction.

We are in danger of destroying truth bit by bit in a phony attempt to weld all religions into one. It is far better to have truth alive and shouting forth above the babble of confusion created by these conflicting claims, than to systematically eliminate all chance of its ever being heard.

To draw attention to these obvious facts about the divided condition of religion and to express opposition to the ecumenical movement is to set off an odd reaction. Churchgoers act amazed and even horrified that anyone would dare suggest that religious differences exist and that some of these differences would have to be classified as error. Religion tries to dismiss those who point out the obvious by classifying them as "bigots" who are full of "prejudice" and "hate." What kind of religious climate are we establishing in these United States?

In the name of unity and the ecumenical movement, many things are expected of everyone. Religious convictions are to be buried under compromise. Religious differences are to be hidden from view. Only those things on which everyone agrees are to be displayed. Religion is to be so broad minded, liberal, and tolerant that everyone can be a part, and no one will be offended. Deep religious convictions are looked upon as weaknesses bred by ignorance.

Anyone who does not conform to this currently popular concept of religion is ostracized as an enemy of society. It is assumed that to differ is to hate. To state that there is a difference in religion and that some of that difference is error, is immediately to be branded a "bigot," described as "prejudiced," and placed in the same category as Communists, the Klu Klux Klan, et cetera.

Why can't we face the fact that it is not necessary to cover religious differences with compromise? Mere acceptance of a maze of contradicting religious claims does not produce unity, just apathy. In the name of religion, above everything else, we should be able to disagree vigorously yet maintain an attitude of love one toward another.

Honesty is a virtue of all religions, and this honesty forces the recognition of difference in religion. To deny this difference requires a measure of hypocrisy, a trait that is contrary to all religions. Deep religious convictions should be encouraged, not disparaged. A truly religious character can only be based on certain, sure, religious convictions. This produces the wonderful assurance we so desperately need. In a world where men's hearts are failing them for fear, we need a sure word, an anchor of the soul. This can only be found in deep, religious convictions that bring peace and assurance. These deep, religious convictions can only come with the certainty that what we believe is the truth. In the religious certainty and assurance that we need there can be no room for doubt. If what we believe is the truth then that which contradicts is error. All religions would have to accept this fact.

Each individual who feels he has the truth of religious peace and assurance also feels the obligation to make it known to others. Although this of necessity involves a clash with what he might believe to be error, it is done in love, not hate. His desire is for the benefit, not harm, of those he seeks to enlighten.

We should be thankful for a religious climate that has allowed us to follow our beliefs and allows everyone else to do the same. This is the kind of religious climate for which we should be striving, not mere conformity to shallow nothingness. A religious freedom that encourages deep religious conviction and aggressive propagation of all religions in peace and love should be our desire.

This is the religious climate that produced rugged faith with tried and proven convictions. It establishes a religious certainty that gives an anchor in this uncertain world. This is what has made America strong. There exists a common bond of love and respect among people with deep, religious convictions, even though they disagree in doctrine.

Chapter 5
Crusade in Complacency

It is an obvious fact that the high ideals, lofty goals, and high-sounding phrases of religion do not find much expression in life. What we say and what we are, seem to be two entirely different things. Our holy crusades are cloaked in contented complacency. The eternal challenge is smothered in the sea of self-satisfaction and buried under the boredom of a lack of interest. The activities of our churches could be described as busy boredom. We are drowsy and yawning at the presentation of truths for which men have gladly died.

The sham and hypocrisy of modern religion is brought into glaring light when we compare what we are with what we sing. Congregational singing is a very important part of the worship services of most churches. Generally, these songs are old familiar hymns that the congregation can sing without too much thought or effort. There is a well-known hymn that is sung by nearly all religions. The average congregation in the average church on an average Sunday morning will be asked to turn in their hymn books to page 46 and stand to sing, "Onward Christian Soldiers." Let's listen as they lift their voices and sing.

"Onward"—This congregation is wandering aimlessly through another dull, humdrum service. The only real goal

33

they have in sight is to get through the service so they can go do something they really enjoy. They look at the clock, count the minutes, and sing, "Onward."

"Christian soldiers"—If there ever was a group that could win a prize for being the least like soldiers it would have to be the average congregation, in the average church, on an average Sunday morning. If our country's safety depended on soldiers such as these, we would surely be in dire circumstances.

"Marching as to war"—When the average congregation, in the average church, on the average Sunday morning sings this phrase, they must surely mean civil war; the only fighting they ever do is among themselves. They are not about to take on an outside enemy. They would rather get along with the real enemy and concentrate on killing off each other.

"With the cross of Jesus, going on before"—The emphasis here surely must be on the phrase, "going on before." Our average congregation has lagged so far behind that the cross of Jesus has gone on out of sight.

"Christ the royal Master, leads against the foe"—The instructions and commands of Christ are clearly laid down and spelled out. They are crisp and clear, but no one seems to pay any attention. This average congregation is calling Christ Master but refusing to submit to Him; they call Him leader and then refuse to follow.

"Forward into battle, see His banners go"—The young pastor learns quickly that it is a near disaster to try to lead his congregation to follow Christ into battle. The last thing they want is anything that looks like controversy or conflict, and the zealous young pastor who goes "forward into battle" is likely to find that he is out there all by himself.

"At the sign of triumph Satan's host doth flee"—Now don't you know that Satan is really trembling at the onslaught of our average sleepy congregation? They must really throw a scare into him. About the only thing he checks out is to make sure they do not pick up the weapons they do have but aren't using. As long as they just shadow box one hour a week he doesn't worry.

"On then, Christian soldiers, on to victory"—The average churchgoer thinks he has won a victory when he struggles out of bed on a Sunday morning, drives to church in his late model car, sits down on a cushioned pew in an air conditioned auditorium and sings, "Onward Christian Soldiers." He thinks of himself as a martyr if the service lasts longer than an hour.

"Hell's foundations quiver at the shout of praise"—If hell is shaking because of this kind of service, it would probably fall apart if an ant stomped by!

"Brothers, lift your voices, loud your anthems raise"—Lift it up now. Everybody sing. Loud singing is the greatest amount of spiritual energy that some churchgoers expend.

"Like a mighty army, moves the church of God"—Think of a mighty army. Now think of the average congregation of reluctant churchgoers. See any resemblance? The only time they look like a mighty army is when they are charging the church parking lot for a quick exit.

The Religion Racket

"Brothers, we are treading where the saints have trod"—The saints of old trod paths that led to being beaten, stoned, and persecuted; their path was one of danger, peril, and sometimes death. Our path is a carpeted aisle down the middle of a fine church.

"We are not divided: all one body we. One in hope and doctrine, one in charity"—Hundreds of warring denominations with contradicting creeds and diverse doctrines have the nerve to sing, "We are not divided." This has to be the height of hypocrisy.

"Onward, then, ye people. Join our happy throng"—A congregation of people comes to church as though they were taking bad medicine: because they think they must. A lot of them are there under protest. The church continually must beg and plead to get them to attend. They sit in church uncomfortable and miserable in spiritual surroundings. This is the group that turns to the world and sings, "Join our happy throng." The world listens and generally responds with, "You've got to be kidding!" Surely we must be!

A look at the words of most of the songs that religious people sing reveals a remarkable contrast. Phrases taken from the songs in a standard hymn book used by thousands of congregations across the land emphasize this difference in what we sing and what we are.

A gentleman arrives at church late. The only reason that he is there is because his wife pestered and badgered him until he finally arose and got ready to attend. Even then, he started to back out, but his children looked at him as if he was Judas Iscariot. He hated having to dress up and would much rather have stayed in bed. He growls and snaps at his family all the way to church. Reluctantly, he slips into a church pew, picks up the hymnal, and joins in singing, "Serve the Lord with gladness."

A church can be split into warring cliques and parties that are engaged in a big church fight, but they'll all stand and sing, "Blest be the tie that binds, our hearts in Christian love." The only time the average churchgoer ever talks of his religion is at church. It embarrasses him for the subject to come up any other place. He sings, "I love to tell the story of Jesus and His glory." A fellow slips a dime into the collection plate and then sings, "Oh, how I love Jesus." People who never prayed more than three minutes at one time in their lives will stand and sing, "Sweet hour of prayer, sweet hour of prayer." The average church constantly has to seek people to sing in the choir. Most people won't respond to the request, yet will join the congregation in singing, "O for a thousand tongues to sing."

Somehow, it seems just a little out of place when the average congregation of proud, sophisticated, cosmopolitan, well-dressed, smug churchgoers stand to sing, "To the old rugged cross, I will ever be true, its shame and reproach gladly bear."

Business meetings of a church can be a real battle. Such meetings could be opened by singing, "The fight is on, O Christian soldier." The same meetings could be closed by singing, "When the battle's over, we shall wear a crown."

A congregation can be full of people who have refused to take an active part in church work; they won't teach, they won't hold an office, they won't serve in any capacity, but they will all stand and sing loudly, "To the work, to the work, we are servants of God."

A woman sits in a congregation seething over a remark someone has made and is carefully plotting her revenge as she sings, "Make me a channel of blessing today." A group that meets and bewails the fact that their pastor is outdated and never deals with current, up-to-date subjects will stand and sing, "Tell me the old, old, story."

This is shallow pretense. To sing songs we obviously do not mean conveys the idea of unreality to all who care to observe. Let's mean what we sing or stop singing.

Then there are the soloists. Yes, there are always the soloists. Generally, these fall into two groups. First, there is always the lady who thinks she can sing and can't. The reason she thinks she can sing is that churchgoers have been lying to her. Anywhere else, people would walk out or tell her to shut up, but in church, we are not as honest as all that; we're too religious. So week after week, this singer keeps up this massacre of music. Everyone smiles and brags on her until she goes through life convinced she can sing.

Secondly, there are the frustrated opera singers. They are thoroughly convinced that if they had been discovered they would have achieved greatness in the music field. They find songs that they feel give full exposure of their voice and continually blast it out into the reluctant ears of a captive church audience, which really prefers a little rock and roll.

Most churches are regularly favored with "specials" by duets, trios, and quartets. These singing groups are usually composed of people who are faithful church workers and are of real value to the church. If their singing group is any good, they will get invitations for guest appearances in other churches. This finally necessitates the group's dropping all their church work in order to be available whenever an invitation to sing is given. Too many times, these "gypsy" singers become cold professionals who have lost their real value.

Chapter 6
Spoiled Saints

The marks of a spoiled child are all too familiar. He gets everything he wants or he throws a temper tantrum, and the parents quickly bow to his wishes. A spoiled child has never been disciplined and, consequently, reacts violently to restrictions. He insists upon having his own way. He has been brought up to be concerned only about himself and has little concern for the feelings of others. Because of overindulgence, it takes something tremendous to please the spoiled child. His demands and expectations become greater and greater, and it takes more and more to keep him happy and satisfied.

The spoiled child finally seems to lose interest in everything. Nothing pleases him and he takes his revenge by making life miserable for everyone around him, particularly his parents. The spoiled child has been petted, pampered, and fawned upon to the degree that love has lost its meaning. His antics and meanness have been smiled at and condoned until he no longer recognizes what is wrong and what is right. The spoiled child has been waited upon hand and foot and cared for to the degree that he has never learned to care for himself or to meet his own simplest needs. Generally, a spoiled child never grows up. He remains a spoiled child all his life. He may finally marry, but he then demands from his wife the same attention he received from his parents.

The Religion Racket

A spoiled child is bad. A spoiled saint is worse. Just as the spoiled child is so prominent in the American family, so is the spoiled saint in the religious world. The allegory is almost perfect. The marks of a spoiled saint are just as familiar as those of a spoiled child.

The spoiled saint must have his own way or he will throw a "temper tantrum." If not everything goes exactly as he thinks it should he'll sulk, pout, and stay home to punish the church for disagreeing with him. His attitude is expressed in the old saying, "If you won't play my way, I'll take my marbles and go home."

A spoiled saint reacts violently to any restrictions. Nobody is going to tell him what he can or cannot do. The spoiled saint is concerned only about himself. "What's in it for me?" seems to be his motto. The spoiled saint has little or no concern for the feelings or well-being of others.

Because of an overindulgence of religious excitement, it takes something tremendous to stir the spoiled saint. Like the spoiled child, his demands and expectations become greater and greater as he demands more and more. Each religious hayride creates an expectation for one that is bigger and better. Finally, he becomes a sophisticated, hardened connoisseur of religious fare and takes great pride in disdainfully rejecting all that is offered. He loses interest in everything, and his only satisfaction seems to be in ruining it for everyone else.

The spoiled saint has been so petted, pampered, and fawned upon by glory-seeking, number-building preachers, and every kind of compromising cult, that he no longer recognizes true love.

Spoiled saints! Waited upon hand and foot by a frightened bunch of professional preachers whose only task seems to be to pamper the whims of this sorry lot. These spoiled saints have long since passed the place of caring for themselves. A spoiled saint never grows up but remains a whimpering, pampered, babied, coddled, spoiled saint throughout his entire life.

What is the cause of this condition? Generally, with few exceptions, a spoiled child is the product of well-meaning but woefully inadequate parents. Others can have a part, but in the final analysis, the responsibility rests with the parents. What about the spoiled saints? Again, the source of this difficulty is not difficult to trace. With few exceptions, it rests with the men who serve as pastors. They are the ones who must ultimately bear the responsibility of raising spoiled saints.

In our day, preaching and pastoring a church has become a highly competitive business. A great number of modern preachers labor under the constant pressure of feeling they must keep the saints happy and content or someone else will lure them away, and they'll be without a job. This is a sorry, despicable picture, but it is an accurate analysis of much of today's religion. So, in the continual effort to please the saints, the process of spoiling progresses. Instead of pastoring his people, the average modern preacher pampers, pets, and coddles them. He gives them everything they want. His main purpose in life seems to be to satisfy every passing whim of his people. He becomes a kind of parasitical politician. A toe-kissing flunky!

The Religion Racket

Modern day religion has raised a crop of saints with no training and no equipment with which to enable them to grow and become strong. Seemingly, there is nothing glamorous and appealing about teaching. It's hard work to teach and hard work to learn, and neither the modern day pastor nor his people have a stomach for this sort of thing.

Today's religion is characterized by an almost complete lack of discipline. Anything goes. The saint is not taught the standards by which he should live. Today, no one expects much of the churchgoer. Is it any wonder he is spoiled and completely unable to determine what course he should follow? The standards have been lowered until there is no longer any difference between the saint and the sinner.

Another contributing factor to the conditions we are describing is that, in a great percentage of religion, entertainment has been substituted for worship. The saint is invited to church, not to worship, but to be entertained. The congregation has become an audience. They don't come to take part: just to watch while a group of high-powered professionals puts on a show.

Each pastor and church feels they must outdo the others to stay in the race of bringing amusement to the saints. On and on the pace goes until the spiritual sensitivities of the goggle-eyed saint become dulled to the extent of being void of understanding. Finally, it will take a good-sized earthquake, four or five erupting volcanoes, and the ominous ticking of a hydrogen bomb to get him even mildly excited.

All the emphasis is upon a religious good time: a hayride of happiness. Get on board, and hallelujah! your troubles are all gone. Just sit back and enjoy yourself. Whatever happened to those good, old, religious words like sacrifice, service, suffering, and self-denial? What's the answer? The situation calls for preachers: real, courageous preachers calling for a repentance that will wake up the slumbering saints. We need preachers who are not afraid to spank the spoiled saint.

Chapter 7
Celestial Competition

There is fierce competition among the different churches and denominations for new members. All these efforts to secure new members come loosely under the title of evangelism. This evangelism takes many forms. One of the most popular is called proselyting. This is the effort put forth to win an individual over from another church or religion. It is generally done privately because publicly it is denounced. It is not officially in the church program, but unofficially it occupies a prominent place. Proselyting is practiced in many different ways.

Anywhere a pastor finds a member of his denomination not attending church, he strongly emphasizes that the individual should attend his church, no matter how far he has to travel. After all, if you are a member of a denomination, you should attend a church of that denomination. However, if a pastor finds a member of another denomination who lives closer to his church, he will emphasize the convenience of attending a church that is close, even if it is another denomination. This matter of convenience is a strong argument and results in many folks changing their religion.

To be able to get across to an individual of another religion the advantages of your religion and the disadvantages of his, without giving an impression of proselyting, is a fine art that is developed by most church workers.

Successful church workers are at a premium and the competition for them is rugged. Generally, the church that offers the most prominent position will win these members. The idea is to emphasize the great need there is in the church for the talent possessed by the sought-after church member. After all, he wouldn't even be missed in the church he now attends and is so desperately needed by the church that is trying to entice him away. Small churches are very successful in raiding larger churches with this type of evangelism.

To keep up a successful program of proselyting, it is necessary to keep the members of all the other local churches informed as to the mistakes and shortcomings of their individual churches. They have a right to know how bad their church is, and when they get the information, it might prompt them to want to change churches. This necessitates each pastor keeping informed about any church trouble or fights that occur in all the other churches because this presents a fine opportunity for evangelism. The group that loses in a church fight is nearly always ready to leave and join another church. The pastor must be careful to court both groups so that no matter who loses he will be looked upon as a friend to whom they can turn.

A church that is going to evangelize successfully must give great emphasis to their "extras." These denominational decoys are set out to attract new members. Generally, it is best to find out what you have that the other churches in the area lack and then go all out in pushing it.

Well-staffed and well-equipped nurseries where parents can leave their children are a big extra that most churches find necessary to have. After all, who wants to go to church with children? Air conditioning is a fine extra and so are cushioned pews. Free transportation is always good. Big parking lots are a must. The church with the shortest services has a big edge over all the other churches. This is a big extra. A successful church must never have services that lap over into prime television time. A youth program with fun and games is always attractive. All these "extras" must be highly advertised along with the guest stars, gospel celebrities, and singing groups who might be appearing.

Evangelism also means the effort that is put forth to win over the unchurched. People not in church are generally harder to enlist. They are not trained in the interpretation of what is really meant by the language that is used in the churches. To the unchurched, there is no apparent difference between themselves and those in the church. So why bother? What's to be gained?

The unchurched listens as everyone praises a Bible that no one is reading and he gets confused. Church people all around him say they love to go to church and yet use every foolish excuse not to attend, and he begins to wonder. He can't understand how prayer is supposed to be the greatest privilege of man, yet he never hears anyone around him praying. He gets confused at the effort put forth in seeking out highly trained preachers to whom no one pays any attention.

When the unchurched does go to church he finds it full of people who don't want to be there and are glad when it's over so they can go do something they are not supposed to enjoy. The only time he ever hears his church-going friends talk about their church is when they are criticizing and belittling it. To say the least, the unchurched is a little confused by this and he is difficult to win. The evangelistic effort generally centers on convincing him that he ought to accept religion, even if it does seem to be phony.

All churches are supposed to be evangelistic. Their commission is to go into all the world and preach the Gospel. Most of the church members carry out at least part of this commission every weekend: they go into all the world. They go to the parks, the beaches, the mountains, camping, boating, et cetera. Some churches become so evangelistic in the summer that they have to shut down. Everybody is gone!

This competition between churches in seeking out new members can make the problem of picking a church to join quite complicated. Most people seem to find it necessary to do a great deal of seeking, or as it might be called, shopping around, before they decide on a church. So many things must be checked. In driving by a church in the summertime, for instance, one can easily see if all the windows are closed. If they are, the building is sure to be air-conditioned. This, of course, is a must.

It is better not to join a church that is in a building program or any other kind of expansion since this always means they will be needing money. The average church member has no desire to be caught up in this kind of thing. It is far better to find a church that someone has paid for and that is already finished.

The first time a family attends church it must be noticed how the people dress. One must never join a church where the people do not dress as well or better than you.

Another thing of extreme importance that must always be checked out before a church is joined is the matter of sin. It is embarrassing to join a church and then find out they condemn the sin you are practicing.

It is always good to check the social standing of the church in the neighborhood. Does it have prestige? Is it where the "right" people attend? Is it accepted by the better class of the neighborhood?

If there is a baby in the family, the church nursery is of vital importance. This is where all those "church diseases" are transmitted.

Does it have a registered nurse in attendance? Does it have those little lights that disinfect? They are nice.

Big roomy parking lots are important. One must be able to arrive late and get away early. Cushioned pews are not an absolute necessity but they are nice. A family will always want to check on the average length of the church services. It is such an annoying thing when services do not stay within a regular time limit. It can disrupt all the other really important plans for the day.

One must always check to be sure the church provides the preferred type of musical entertainment. This is important to the rock and roll enthusiast. It is always good, if there are teenagers in the family, to check out the young people's program. Do they have regularly scheduled dances? Do they have a good recreation program? Do they show good movies? Do they have parties?

One must be very careful about the pastor of a church. Of course, he must be well educated, well dressed, experienced, and a good mixer. He must be a young 35. (Preachers find it necessary to be a young 35 all their lives. This is a little difficult. This is the age when he is supposedly able to still appeal to the young people and also reach the older folks.

It must be determined before one joins a church that the preacher is not one who is going to be expecting a lot out of anyone who belongs to his church. Some preachers expect their members to get involved in the things of religion and this can be a real drag. The preacher must not be a crusader; that is one of those fellows who is always taking a stand on some issue and calling upon everyone else to do likewise. This can be embarrassing.

Many folks find it good not to join a church close to their home. If they live a good distance from the church, they feel they can't be expected to participate in too many different activities at the church. Usually, it is preferred that a church not be too zealous. After all, who wants their children growing up to be religious fanatics and going off to Africa as missionaries?

If a family has an eligible daughter it is well to check to see if there are any eligible young men. Church is a fine place to do a little match making. If you have a boy, of course, you check out the girls.

Of course, some folks never join a church. Every Sunday they just visit a church. They are perpetual visitors. This has its advantages since it enables them to reap all the benefits of church-going without having to pay any of the cost or assume any of the responsibilities. Like a parasite, a parish parasite.

New members always receive a lot of attention and everyone goes out of their way to please and greet them. Many folks like this so much they stay new members. Every time the newness wears off they join another church and they are new again. They just tramp from one church to another; that's it. They are church tramps!

Of course, what the church believes, what it teaches, and its spirituality are important, but the average churchgoer feels these things can be fitted in if everything else checks out.

Chapter 8
Child Neglect

How to "reach the young people" is a constant problem of religion, and the facts reveal the enormity of this difficulty. The greater percentage of young people are not attending church and Sunday school, and those who are, generally drop out somewhere in their early teens. Most of the frantic effort "to reach the young people" is in reality an attempt to retrieve what religion has already lost.

All religion knows that if it is going to be successful it must make provision for the teaching and training of children in spiritual things. This is of supreme importance. The simple, spiritual truth must be planted in the fertile minds and hearts of the young. The teaching agency of most churches is called a Sunday school, Bible school, or church school. Normally, it consists of one hour set aside on Sunday morning for the purpose of teaching. About 20 to 25 minutes of this hour is usually given to opening exercises, singing, record keeping, announcements, promotions, et cetera, and another 5 to 10 minutes is consumed in changing from assembly rooms to classrooms. This leaves about 30 minutes for actual teaching. Thirty minutes a week! This compares to 30 hours a week the same student spends in public school. In public school, he attends class more in one week than he does the whole year in Sunday school.

The Religion Racket

By the time the student graduates from high school, he will have the equivalent of 12 weeks of religious training. This is less than one semester, and only a small percentage is getting this amount. And we wonder why we are a generation of spiritual ignoramuses! Nowhere do we deceive ourselves more than when we try to make believe that the teaching a child receives in Sunday school is enough to give him the spiritual education he so desperately needs.

Our public school teachers are professionals: well trained and qualified. The Sunday school, however, must depend upon volunteers, and this presents some problems. The average Sunday school is constantly in need of Sunday school teachers. There always seems to be a shortage, but very few are willing to take upon themselves this responsibility. This necessitates using whoever is available, whether they are qualified or not. This results in too large a percentage of Sunday school teachers being unqualified and incapable of teaching. Too often, they will waste the 30 precious minutes out of the week the child is given to learn spiritual things.

Children are quick to recognize the inefficiency and inabilities of these teachers and are ready to take advantage. Too often, a Sunday school class is just 30 minutes of utter confusion with a harassed teacher helplessly trying, at the least, to keep order. The unreliability of Sunday school teachers is proverbial. A large percentage of these teachers seem to have utterly no recognition of the importance of what they are doing. They will show up late, unprepared, and will think nothing of being absent without making provision for their class. The sight of a departmental superintendent searching frantically around a Sunday school for a substitute teacher is an all too familiar one.

In some instances, the Sunday school is used mainly as a promotional organization designed to get large numbers to attend church and Sunday school. So much time is given to getting a good number present that there is no time left to teach them after they are there. It is common to see attendance contests take up most of the teaching time. If this weren't so tragic, it would be funny.

Every good Sunday school must have good officers. Good superintendents and departmental heads with their assistants and secretaries are a necessity. These offices are mostly filled by folks who have proven themselves good, educated teachers. This means that the best teachers are put into positions where they don't teach. Then they spend their time trying to get the job done with teachers who can't teach but must be used anyway.

Possibly nowhere does the child cry out for firm guidance more than in religion, and nowhere else does he find such a deaf ear. There are two scenes that, in all probability, are etched into the memory of everyone who has ever caught the vision of the importance of religious training for children. One of these scenes is a young child whose interest and wonder about spiritual things has been stirred, and he eagerly anticipates Sunday morning when he can attend Sunday school where these wonders are unfolded. When Sunday morning comes, the parents concoct some foolish excuse and keep the child home. The interest dies, and the glow of wonder fades out, sometimes forever.

The Religion Racket

The other scene is a room full of children gathered in a Sunday school class eagerly awaiting those precious moments of spiritual training, and the teacher comes in late and unprepared or doesn't even show up. This kind of damage is irreparable and can even be eternal.

With this type of training, it is small wonder that the child, at a very early age, becomes aware of the sham and hypocrisy of religion. A sincere, honest child will want to know. He will look for answers: answers he never gets. He grows up firmly convinced no one has ever really leveled with him about religion. By far, the large percentage of the youth of today receives no religious training in their home, their school, or their church. No wonder they can dismiss it as of no importance.

Those exposed to the teaching offered in the average church are quick to sense the unreality of it all: the pretense and hypocrisy. They get a glimpse of the truth, but when they compare it with what they see practiced they generally reject it in disgust. A child is not as easily deceived as we might think. Early in his life, he becomes aware of the difference between what he hears in church and what he sees in his parents. He is conscious of the vast superiority of his public school over his Sunday school. He is acutely conscious of the habitual hypocrisy all around. He feels he is being deceived. No one is really laying it on the line. By the time the child reaches an age of independent decision, he is intensely aware of his spiritual need. He is also aware that the religion to which he has been exposed does not meet that need. He then turns to something else.

Sometimes, in order to show his contempt for the pretense and sham of religion, he will run to what he feels is an extreme opposite. He will find satisfaction in opinions, fashions, and actions that are contradictory to all for which he believes religion stands. He delights in shocking the generation that has tried to impose upon him their hypocrisies. He excuses his wrong actions simply because they are done in honesty and sincerity as opposed to covering the same actions under the veneer of religion. He speaks of a "new morality" when he never really knew anything about the old. He expresses himself in what he believes are unorthodox opinions, appearances, clothing, music, literature, et cetera. His rebellion is nothing more than a desire to be the opposite of that to which he objects. He recognizes a need but doesn't know how it is to be satisfied. He may ultimately try to expand his mind with drugs and indulge in every excess which lust dictates. He fails because religion failed.

There are others who seem to be able to reject religion with a contempt that only great wisdom can have for ignorance. They fancy themselves as having intellectually advanced beyond a need of religion. They condone it in others of lesser knowledge and wait impatiently for them to catch up. A young person comes to this conclusion about the time he is a sophomore in college.

Some of the young will turn to new exotic cults that all established religions condemn. The new cult is attractive only because it is condemned. The majority just ignore religion as of no importance. Others drift into the sham and hypocrisy of their parents. Each generation gets farther away. And time is running out.

Chapter 9
The Cupid Cult

It is the responsibility of religion to provide instruction that will enable the child to grow into a mature adult equipped to distinguish between right and wrong. Religion offers the training that brings the individual into a right relationship with his fellow man. Religion sets the guidelines and standards that govern the conduct between a man and woman. These moral guidelines bring happiness, maturity, and respect.

Nowhere is the failure of religion more evident than in its lack of influence upon the morality of America. The standards and moral guidelines of religion are scoffed at and ignored by this generation. Religion's failure has resulted in a generation that has failed to grow up morally. Its attitude toward right conduct in sex relations remains childish and immature. They may become adult in years but remain adolescent in morals.

This moral immaturity has resulted in this generation acting as if they were the first to discover the difference between the male and female. They are a little overwhelmed by the whole thing because they haven't really determined how to act in the face of this discovery. Formerly, this problem was dealt with in the early teens, but not anymore. It has become a constant difficulty. It may be that this nation is suffering from perpetual pubescence. It is characterized by the same immaturity, uncertainty, and anxieties. Normally, it would be expected that this constant obsession with sex would bring about some form of maturity. This has not happened. This generation has prolonged the agony of adolescence indefinitely.

This infantile attitude toward sex has created many problems. Juvenile fantasy has exaggerated sex beyond any resemblance of reality. Since this make-believe world is never realized, the individual lives in a constant state of frustration and failure.

The childishness of today's generation concerning sex makes them extremely vulnerable to exploitation. They are bombarded on every hand by appeals to the sex instinct. Business has been quick to recognize the opportunity of selling its products by coming up with a "sexy" image. This has resulted in "sexy" automobile tires, "sexy" toothpaste, "sexy" breakfast cereals, deodorants, razors, et cetera. Just about everything is sold with a sex image.

These agitated adolescents find their inadequacies create an insatiable desire for exposure to nudity. This is always an indication of a callow concept of sex. It has resulted in practically everything about us being reduced to wanton vulgarity. Nudity has become the main commodity peddled in magazines, movies, nightclubs, television, stage shows, books, et cetera. Each depth of depravity that is reached only produces a demand for more. Sex perversion is popular, licentiousness is longed for, and obscenity is adored!

The Cupid Cult

To the Romans, the god of sensual love was called Cupid. The Greeks knew this god as Eros. In America, we do not have an original name for him, but the god of sensual love has more worshippers than any other god. The Roman god of Cupid was originally pictured as a fine specimen of a mature young male. This image degenerated into that of a pudgy adolescent. This probably is more closely related to today's worshippers of a sensual god. Possibly, they could be identified as the Cupid Cult. Sex love has been elevated into a cult. Love, sex appeal, and uncontrolled passion have become the prime factor in practically every phase of our complex, modern life.

Lately, there have been some attempts to spell out the doctrines of this Cupid Cult. These doctrines come loosely under the heading of what is called "the new morality." It really isn't new. It has been dredged up from the sewers of past ages where it sank under the weight of its own fetid mass. Today's effort is nothing more than an attempt to return to the childish concepts of the primitives. It is not a step forward but a step backward.

This Cupid Cult would have us kick aside all of the "old morality" with its restrictions and emphasis upon right and wrong. Permissiveness is the key word. If both parties agree, wrong becomes right. Sex relations are heralded as an expression of love that is not to be limited to marriage. Marriage is outdated. Sex relations ultimately will become as casual as a handshake!

In this "new morality," the idea of right and wrong is ridiculed. Each individual sets his own standards and is not to be influenced by anything other than his own conscience. Any mature reasoning knows this sounds good but that it doesn't work. It must be remembered that this generation seemingly has no desire to reach maturity in morals or intellect.

It is evident that this religion is very successful in America. The adherents are dedicated to the worship of sex love. They do not have church buildings as such, but congregate in theaters and drive-in movies to bow before the latest sex symbol. Here, they receive the inspiration and stimulation to pursue the goal of their religion, the satisfaction of lust. In the drive-in movies, what is portrayed on the screen is quickly practiced in the cars. They watch as their "sex kittens" give graphic illustrations of what is accepted as the ideal life. They are called "sex kittens," probably because they have the face of an angel and the morals of an alley cat. What is displayed upon the silver screen has more influence upon the morals of America than what is preached from the pulpits of all other religions combined.

The "Bible" of this religion is the philosophy that can be gleaned from the current issue of magazines whose main features are pictures of nudes. The philosophy seems to urge men to stay boys all their life and to spend their time in play rather than to assume the responsibility of adults. The novel that can describe sex in the foulest language is always a big influence. The music of the Cupid Cult is given mainly to relating amateurish exploits in sex. The young seem to find this music very stimulating and challenging.

Again, it must be said that the success of the Cupid Cult emphasizes the failure of religion. This generation finds it easy to cast aside the "old morality" simply because they never really knew what it was. We spend billions of dollars providing the education that will enable this generation to comprehend and eventually master all the complexities of modern life. All, that is, except morality. Religion has failed to provide the foundation that enables a child to reach maturity in morals. It is a small wonder that the young are taken in by any raving reprobate that happens on the scene. Religion has offered no alternative.

The only moral strength this generation has is what has seeped down from previous generations. Religion today has deserted the field of battle and seemingly run up the white flag of surrender. The ultimate in humiliation is the way some religions are willing to embrace the Cupid Cult and accept its standards for their own.

Chapter 10
Do-It-Yourself Religion

Nearly everyone has heard the story of the minister on the golf course who sliced his drive off the first tee toward the rough. The ball hit a tree, ricocheted to the ground, hit a rock, and bounded back into the air. On its flight upward, the ball hit a bird in flight just at the right angle and bounced onto the green, rolling to a stop one inch from the hole. A gentle wind blew it into the cup. A hole in one! The minister raised his eyes to heaven and complained, "Father! Please! I'd rather do it myself."

This is not only amusing, but also illustrates a truth. In matters of religion, most people seem to prefer doing it themselves. We have developed a kind of "do-it-yourself" religion. The prophets spoke of every man doing that which was right in his own eyes and this is a description of today. Each individual seems to have his own particular idea of religion that he is building from a do-it-yourself kit. We never seem to be content with what God has said or done. We'd rather do it ourselves.

Nothing is more apparent than the uncomplicated simplicity of worship as it was practiced in New Testament times. Obviously, this was to be the pattern, but it has never satisfied man; he'd rather do it himself. Most of the elaborate, ornate, complicated rituals and procedures of today's worship came from man's do-it-yourself kit. One would be hard pressed to try to associate the pompous, formal, ritualistic ceremonies of today's religion with an example given by the Lord. We'd just rather do it ourselves in our own way. We want to be religious, but we don't want the Lord to tell us how.

Much of today's religion is founded upon do-it-yourself creeds and doctrines. Jesus put it this way, "But in vain do they worship me, teaching for doctrines the commandments of men" (Matt. 15:9).

Religion has developed its own methods for getting things done. Everyone seems to have his own schemes, systems, and methods for being religiously successful. "How to do it" books on just about any subject are available. A casual look at the books on religion reveals a great number with titles such as the following:

How to Boost Your Church Attendance

How to Work for Christ

How to Win Others to Christ

How to Be a Soul Winner

How to Succeed in the Christian Life

1000 Plans and Ideas for Sunday School Workers

65 Ways to Give an Evangelistic Invitation

Ideas for a Successful Church Program

Successful Church Publicity

These books all present what are supposed to be tried and proven plans for being religiously successful. They might be called "get religious quick" schemes. They are the do-it-your-selfer's dream. These schemes all come packaged, complete with elaborate details as to how to make them work. If the plan is followed, results are guaranteed!

There are those alert enough to keep an eye on the advertising, business, and entertainment world. Anything that works in these fields can usually be religionized and made to work in the churches. Too much of religion is concerned with carrying out success schemes and promotions. We have taken the majesty, glory, and magnificence of religion and reduced it to a cheap, do-it-yourself plan.

Yes, do-it-yourself religion is popular. Everyone prays, "Thy will be done." However, really, we would rather do it ourselves. Everyone can know what the Bible says, but we'd still rather do it our own way. The preacher brings good sermons, but we are not about to receive his instructions. We would rather do it ourselves.

Another very apparent quality that early worship services possessed was a lack of organizational machinery. Not so in today's do-it-yourself religion. Look at the mass of complex organizational machinery we have found necessary to run our do-it-yourself religion. An overabundance of organization bogs down the whole structure. The average denomination has to operate in a complicated hierarchy that is awesome to behold.

The program of the church is normally carried on through a maze of committees, boards, departments, et cetera. Very little ever really gets done because it is almost impossible for any project to work its way through all the organizational channels. This reaches the extent that nearly all the members of some churches are officers in the church machinery. Too many chiefs and not enough Indians!

The church is nearly always a member of a local denominational organization, which in turn is part of a still larger one. This proceeds until it reaches the worldwide activities. The organizations in these various branches of the denomination continually grow larger, usually by duplication of labor. Ordinarily, the denomination belongs to one of the super world organizations that bind the denominations together. One of these super organizations employs more than 200 ministers in desk jobs at its headquarters! The average pastor could probably give himself full-time to keeping up with all the organizational machinery of which his position makes him a part. Too many times, he finds this is what has happened.

The complex machinery of today's religion has also produced a need for spiritual specialists. There was a time when being a minister meant preaching and attending to the spiritual needs of a congregation. Today the cry is for specialization. The day of the general practitioner will probably soon be over. Today it is common for larger churches to have several different kinds of clergy on their ordained staffs. One minister can be in charge of sermons, another specializes in home visitations, while another heads up the ministry of teaching. There are educational directors, music directors, and pastoral counselors, who also operate clinics. In some cases, there are even women preachers, but these find it difficult to meet the requirement of being the husband of one wife.

Missionaries have to be experts in irrigation, social work, nutrition, contour plowing, construction, languages, et cetera. Missionaries have found that a lot of their work has been taken over by the Peace Corps. Some have found this gives them little time to do such non-essential things as teaching the Bible.

Most of the activity in religion today is nothing more than keeping the machinery running. A lot of this organizational machinery is kept running long after its purpose has been forgotten. The resultant mess that man has made of religion reveals the utter failure of this complicated mass of organizational machinery. The simple solution seems to be to admit the failure, scrap the machinery, and turn the Lord's business back over to the Lord!

Today's do-it-yourself religion has even developed a language all its own. It is composed of words and phrases that never mean what they say. These words and phrases have to be translated, or at least, interpreted. Most churchgoers understand this language and the meanings have been fairly well standardized. Here are some typical phrases and their interpretations:

"And in conclusion…"
Interpretation: "I am going to preach another 20 minutes."

"This is a really fine crowd for such a rainy morning."
Interpretation: "The attendance is way down."

The Religion Racket

"Now I never argue about religion."
Interpretation: "I'm going to set you straight about religion."

"Now I don't want to pass judgment."
Interpretation: "Here is my judgment."

"Now I don't want to talk about them."
Interpretation: "Wait until you hear what I heard about them."

"I don't believe in offering envelopes because the Scriptures say, 'let not thy left hand know what thy right hand doeth' (Matt. 6:3)."
Interpretation: "I'm ashamed to let anyone know how little I give."

"Now I don't want my children to get special attention."
Interpretation: "My kids are better than the others."

"One thing about it, he really sings from the heart."
Interpretation: "He can't sing."

"I believe in allowing my children to express themselves fully. I don't believe we should lay down too many restrictions. Young people must have their fun."
Interpretation: "My children are running out of control. I can't do a thing with them."

"It's not the amount of the gift; it is the spirit that counts."
Interpretation: "I'm ashamed to give you this little gift."

"Now I know what I say doesn't amount to much."
Interpretation: "You had better listen to me."

"It doesn't matter if you win or lose, it's how you play the game that counts."
Interpretation: "We lost."

"After all, confession is good for the soul."
Interpretation: "I got caught."

"Sure, I take a little drink now and then."
Interpretation: "I'm a drunk."

"Let's adjourn the meeting and think about it for a week."
Interpretation: "Let's go home and see what our wives say."

"I won't make promises I might not keep, but I'll try to be in church Sunday."
Interpretation: "I won't be in church Sunday."

"All that preacher is after is money."
Interpretation: "I'm not giving."

"I don't believe the pastor should be so personal in his preaching."
Interpretation: "I'm guilty."

"I don't care what people say about me."
Interpretation: "It kills me when I think people are talking about me."

"The preacher shouldn't have favorites."
Interpretation: "The preacher is not paying enough attention to me."

"I don't think she would be happy in our church."
Interpretation: "Don't invite her."

Chapter 11
Hollow Holidays

Most religions in the United States use Sunday, the first day of the week, as a day of worship. This is called the Lord's Day. What happens on this day is a real indicator of the place that religion holds in this country.

We can see the decline since the majority of churches have just one service a week. And that is discontinued many times in the summer months. The routine of churches in this country originally included a lot more services. There were always Sunday school and morning worship services on Sunday mornings. There was a time of studying, preaching, praising, worshipping, et cetera. Everyone would return on Sunday nights for evening worship. This was a worship service characterized by a great emphasis on evangelism. Added to these was the mid-week prayer meeting, ordinarily on Wednesday. The church would assemble for a time of worship, praise, and prayer. There was a time when most churches would assemble on Saturday night in preparation for Sunday.

What have been mentioned are the "regular services" that were held every week. In addition, churches would have revival meetings of anywhere from one week to a month or more, and folks came every night! Throughout the year, there would be Bible conferences, training courses, et cetera. Religion meant something then. What happened?

The first to go was probably the Saturday night meetings. Folks found other things they would rather do on Saturday, things that were not quite so religious. The next casualty was the mid-week prayer meeting. As they became more self-sufficient, they found they didn't need to pray as much. Besides, it took so much time. Sunday evening services lasted a little longer but finally fell by the wayside. After all, folks didn't want to be fanatical about their religion, and there were so many other things clamoring for attention. Along the way, revival meetings went out of style and were dropped, along with all similar services. This left Sunday morning services, and they are just barely holding on. Already, many churches are closing down tight during the summer months. On any given Sunday morning, there are more church members not attending church than are attending. How long?

Religious folks seem to find no inconsistency in using the Lord's Day as a day of play, visiting, loafing, et cetera. More and more it is just another workday. More and more businesses are open on Sunday. Less and less it is the Lord's Day. How long?

We have condensed our religion to an occasional one hour service on Sunday morning, and that still seems to be too much. Some have it down to two a year: Christmas and Easter! These are the two really big days on the religious calendar: Christmas and Easter. There are other holidays, but these two are by far the most important.

Christmas is supposed to be the celebration of the birth of Christ. This explanation is needed because it can hardly be recognized as such from the way it is observed. This celebration of the birthday of Christ didn't start until about three or four hundred years after His birth, but it has come a long way since.

Christmas supposedly is a time of "peace on earth and good will towards men." It is a time of expressing our love one toward another in gift-giving. At Christmas, we are supposed to be particularly aware of spiritual values, and our minds and hearts are to be attuned to our Savior in a wonderful time of closeness and fellowship.

That Christmas is not all it is supposed to be is very evident. Every year we hear the familiar cries about putting Christ back into Christmas. We are admonished not to forget the real meaning of Christmas. Every year the same petitions go forth, but no one really pays much attention.

Actually, what is Christmas? Christmas is large crowds of greedy shoppers, tired and short-tempered, jamming the stores in a spending spree that grows bigger every year.

Christmas is sending Christmas cards. This is a very unique custom. About the only attention these cards really get is to be counted. You judge how well you are liked by how many cards you receive. In order to get cards you must send cards, and this necessitates maintaining an ever-increasing list of names and addresses of folks who are obligated to send you a card because you sent them one. This way you get lots of cards and everyone will know you have a lot of friends with whom you are popular. If you receive more cards than you mail, you are something really special.

Christmas is spending a fortune on Christmas trees and decorations that have no spiritual significance. Christmas is kindling greed in a child's heart. A youngster who is already overindulged will sit down on Christmas morning and rip through one package after another and always he seems to have an expression on his face that says, "Is that all I got?"

Christmas is the birthday of Christ, and Santa Claus gets all the attention. The question is, "Do you believe in Santa Claus?" not, "Do you believe in Jesus Christ?"

Christmas is taking back all those gifts, which were just what you needed and exchanging them. Christmas is a time of office parties and other types of drunken orgies. It is a time when it is supposed to be all right to make love to your secretary and your neighbor's wife.

Christmas is reveling in the name of religion, where drunkenness is substituted for devotion, and where there is more greed than God. Christmas is doing for the needy once a year what we should be doing all year. Christmas is using the money we have saved all year in a Christmas club to buy everyone gifts they don't need and probably won't use.

In view of the covetousness, greed, drunkenness, reveling, and hypocrisies that bury Christmas, maybe we need to change our slogan. Instead of trying to put Christ in Christmas maybe we should take Christ out of Christmas. Let it be what it is and quit disguising it as a religious holy day.

Then there is Easter. Each church probably has its largest attendance on Easter. It seems everyone goes to church on Easter. Easter is the day when the resurrection of Christ is celebrated. The resurrection of Christ presents the prospects of victory over death. The symbol of this day is an Easter bunny bringing hen eggs. Easter, as everybody knows, is the time to buy new clothes and strut to church in the Easter parade.

It doesn't seem to strike anyone as particularly odd that the wild, depraved, drunken orgy that takes place in New Orleans every year is associated with Easter.

How handicapped it would be to celebrate victory over death one hour a year, yet this is what a great percentage of church-goers are supposed to be content doing. What we really are putting on display at Easter is not our new clothes but our old shams and hypocrisies.

It seems that real religion would insist that the tainted hands of greed, commercialism, and drunken reveling be taken off what are supposed to be holy days.

Chapter 12
Wishy-Washy Warriors

Moses had died and Joshua had assumed leadership of the congregation of Israel. Joshua's main task was to lead his congregation into Canaan and possess the land. After crossing Jordan, the first big obstacle that Joshua and his people faced was the strong, fortified city of Jericho.

God gave Joshua the instructions on how he was to conquer the city of Jericho. Joshua was to line up his congregation with the armed men going first, followed by seven priests with trumpets. Next in line was the ark of the Lord, which was to be followed by all the people. Every day this procession was to march around the city of Jericho one time. The seven priests were to blow their trumpets each day, but all the people were to remain silent. They were to do this for six days. On the seventh day, they were to walk around the city seven times, and on the seventh trip, the priests were to blow the trumpets, and the people were to shout a great shout. The Lord's promise was that the walls of the city would fall down flat and a great victory would be theirs.

Joshua, the new leader of the congregation, had to carry these instructions to his people. This is a striking picture. It would be interesting to know what kind of reaction the congregation of Israel expressed to these unusual commands. It would be more interesting to try to contemplate what kind of reaction a modern congregation would have to the instructions given by Joshua. Let's try to picture it. Joshua has just given his instructions on how to take Jericho. How would a modern congregation react?

Typical reaction #1: "Well, I'll tell you one thing. Joshua is not like Moses, our old pastor. Moses would have had more sense than to try to take a city with a stupid plan like that. Joshua just hasn't had enough experience. Before we make fools out of ourselves, we had better form a pulpit committee and start looking for a new pastor: one like Moses."

Typical reaction #2: "Now, I just don't see why we have to march around the city seven days. If we are going to take it, why not do it today? Why wait seven days? That's a big waste of time."

Typical reaction #3: "Line up and march around the city blowing trumpets! That's no way to capture a city! Anybody knows that much. What we have to do is get better organized. We will form a steering committee to lay the framework for a 'Society for Knocking Down Walls.' I'll serve as chairman."

Typical reaction #4: "That's not the way we used to do it. I don't trust these new ideas of Joshua's. If we are going to take Jericho we will have to use the 'old-fashioned' ways. Now when Moses wanted to cross the Red Sea he just held out his stick over the sea, and when he wanted water from the rock, he hit it with a stick. I say if we are going to capture Jericho we are going to have to get some sticks and start hitting the wall."

Typical reaction #5: "Now, I don't hold with Joshua's plan, but I can't go along with this crowd that wants to knock down Jericho's walls with sticks. One time when we were in a battle and we were being beaten, our old pastor Moses held up his hands and we started to win. When he got tired and his hands came down, we again suffered defeat. Finally, Aaron and Hur took hold of Moses' arms and held them up and the victory was ours. I don't care what Joshua said. Tomorrow we ought to get out there and hold his hands up. We'll need at least three men. One to hold Joshua and one each for his arms. This will get the job done."

Typical reaction #6: "I suppose Joshua knows what he's doing, but you can count me out. I see no sense in getting up before dawn. I've got to get my sleep. We could start this thing at noon just as easily. Tomorrow's the only day I get to take it easy and I'm not about to get up that early."

Typical reaction #7: "Now I wouldn't mind getting up and marching around Jericho one day, but seven days! That's too much. Joshua is trying to turn us into a group of fanatics. One day out of seven is enough. It's none of his business what we do with the other six."

Typical reaction #8: "I'd tell Joshua just as soon as I'd tell you: I'm not going to march in that parade around Jericho. I'm unalterably opposed to the entire plan. It's doomed to failure. Did you see those seven men he picked to blow the trumpets? That's favoritism. Why, I can play a trumpet better than any of them. No sir. Count me out."

Typical reaction #9: "You see? What did I tell you? We got up and marched around Jericho a whole day and nothing happened. I knew it wouldn't work. There is absolutely no sense in going on with this for six more days. It didn't work today and it won't work then."

Typical reaction #10: "I'm not going to get out there and march around that city. I'm a singer, not a soldier."

Typical reaction #11: "I've called all of you other ladies together to form this discussion group. We need to go thoroughly into Joshua's plan for capturing Jericho. I'm sure all of you are familiar with this plan, but there are some things of which you may not be aware. You all know about the march around the city, the trumpets, the ark, et cetera. But did you hear what else Joshua said? Well, he said not 'to make any noise with your voice, neither shall any word proceed out of your mouth.' Now that's censorship. Joshua must think he is a dictator. Well, I'll tell you one thing and I'm sure you ladies will agree. I'm not going to keep quiet for six days. I don't care what Joshua might think, I'm going to have my say."

Typical reaction #12: "I've been an officer in this army for a long time. I was here before Joshua came along. I'm going to sit back and let some of the younger fellows take over. Besides, I might get my uniform dirty marching around that city."

Typical reaction #13: "What do we need Jericho for anyway? We have a nice little congregation, and things haven't been going too bad. Why don't we just settle down and wait awhile? Jericho isn't going anywhere. After a while, if we still want to, we can always capture the city. What's the big rush? Let's think it over."

Typical reaction #14: "What's all this going to cost? Our treasury is already low. Joshua is going to run us so far in debt we'll never get out."

Typical reaction #15: "Boy! That Joshua! He's something else. Can you imagine what those people in Jericho are going to think when we take this ragtag mob and march around their city? They'll laugh us all the way back to Egypt. They'll think we're crazy. What we need to do is send a delegation into Jericho and work out an agreement. These people are just like us. Let's get together with them and stop all the fighting. The way I hear it, things are pretty good inside Jericho. I wouldn't mind joining up with them. How about you?"

Typical reaction #16: "The one thing I don't like about Joshua's plan is that he doesn't have enough music. Think of it. Just seven trumpets for the whole congregation. Personally, I could do with less talking from Joshua and more playing from the trumpets."

Typical reaction #17: "All my life I've been training to use a sword and shield, and now Joshua comes along and says I'm not going to need them to take Jericho. I don't know about the rest of you, but when he's out there marching around the city, I'm going to be right here polishing my shield and sharpening my sword. I know what I can do with them, and I'll trust that any day before I would Joshua's plan."

Typical reaction #18: "If I understand it right, we are not supposed to take any of the gold and silver out of Jericho for ourselves. If this is so, what I want to know is, what are we going to get out of it? What's in it for us? Joshua can't expect us to go out there for nothing. I bet he's going to get his."

The Religion Racket

It doesn't take much to see that if Joshua's congregation would have reacted in this manner he would have had a crushing defeat rather than the glorious victory he did experience. It certainly pictures to us why religion is failing today.

Chapter 13
Sanctified Sin

One of the difficult things, which a supposedly religious people have had to cope with, is how to be religious and sinful at the same time. This presents quite a problem because most religions inconveniently identify right and wrong, and some even go so far as to commend the good and condemn the evil!

This attempt to be sinful and religious simultaneously has produced some ingenious efforts. One of the truly sophisticated ways of accomplishing this is to pretend doubt and ask for a definition of terms. What is good? What is evil? This works well because, of course, as is already known, there is some confusion as to the meaning of these terms, and this confusion gives an excuse for continuing in sin. After all, who says it is sin? Maybe what is sin for you is not sin for me? When this confusion is created, it is a big help in enabling one to be sinful and religious at the same time.

If one wants to go to the trouble, he can usually find a church that doesn't condemn any of his particular sins. This is a great help in getting over the obstacle of being both sinful and religious. A little more difficult, but very effective, is the effort to draw a line of distinction between spiritual things and material things. This finally narrows down to being religious at church and sinful everywhere else. Most people find this an agreeable arrangement.

If one has the time, he can join efforts with some supposedly intellectual group that is working on a philosophy of religion that will completely reverse the meaning of religious terms. They call good evil, and evil good. Right becomes wrong and wrong becomes right. Most people find it easier to live by these terms. One has to be a little careful, though. A man named Isaiah, about 2,700 years ago, wrote, "Woe unto them that call evil good, and good evil; that put darkness for light, and light for darkness; that put bitter for sweet, and sweet for bitter!" (Isa. 5:20). He could be right.

There is another method used in the attempt to be religious and sinful concurrently, but it is not quite as honest and above-board as the others are. In fact, it's downright sneaky, but is used a lot. This simply involves being religious and denying you are sinful when in the presence of your religious friends, and being sinful and denying you are religious while around your sinful friends. This can be complicated, particularly when you keep meeting your religious friends in sinful places and your sinful friends in religious places.

Another system that has grown popular in recent years is to religionize sin. Sin is taken out of the world, brought over into the church, and sanctified. Sanctified sin! This, supposedly, makes it all right and it enables one to sin...religiously.

Some people, coping with the problem of being both sinful and religious, employ an action called backsliding. These people will alternate being religious and being sinful. They are never really religious and sinful at the same time, but it accomplishes about the same thing. After being religious for a time, they will backslide and be sinful for a while. After a while, they will return and again be religious. This is an accepted, standard procedure and has the added advantage of always being joyfully welcomed back whenever one returns, either to his sinful friends or to his religious friends.

There are those who use what might be called a diversionary action. This is really very simple. You pick out a sin you are not practicing and vigorously condemn it. An all out crusade is launched against this sin. Everyone becomes so engrossed in fighting the uncommitted sin that no one pays any attention to the sins being committed. This, of course, is a great aid to maintaining both sin and religion. If a preacher wants to condemn sin, he has to find one his congregation is not practicing. Throwing babies to crocodiles as an act of worship is a sin that gets a lot of condemnation.

Another diversionary action is to put all the emphasis upon the minute interpretation of some obscure religious doctrine. When this is done with great zeal, little attention is paid to sin. If a religion will cooperate by softening its emphasis upon the distinction between right and wrong, the two finally blend. Being religious and sinful at the same time becomes an easy thing.

The modern idea that it is wrong to place any prohibitions upon children can be used. We are told that to place any restrictions upon children is harmful. It can cause frustrations, inhibitions, and a host of other horrible things. They must be allowed full expression. This means that the children can sin if they want, and this necessitates the parents following the same path. After all, we want to do right for our children even if it's wrong!

Men have found it is good to keep religion in their wife's name. How much more religious can you be than to see that your wife and children are provided for in religious matters? This enables the man to continue his sinning with a clear conscience.

Chapter 14
By Popular Demand

Instead of meeting the demands of God, religion has been changed to meet the demands of the public. It seems that religion is back by popular demand. This has resulted in religion being diluted, streamlined, whipped-up, condensed, smoothed, and made palatable to the religious tastes of the public. This kind of religion has become popular. It is sweeping the country. Jukeboxes grind out the latest popular gospel tunes. Movie magazines carry news of the religious activities of the movie stars. More money is coming into religious treasuries than ever before, and great new church buildings are continually being built. A greater percentage of folks belong to churches than ever before in history. Tremendous evangelistic campaigns are regularly held with thousands in attendance, and great numbers of decisions are recorded. Quite regularly, the current best seller is a book on religion. The newspapers and magazines carry regular columns by religious writers, and the radio and television carry religious programs. Religious colleges, universities, high schools, and elementary schools are multiplying rapidly. This type of religion is booming. The cry of "revival" is heard repeatedly.

In the haste to get everybody aboard the bandwagon, a carnival spirit has developed. The bands are playing, the flags are flying, and everyone is invited to a hayride of happiness, a religious romp. Popcorn, peanuts, and paper hats! Our religious boom today is a little like cotton candy and bubble gum. It seems big and beautiful until you get your teeth into it and find it dissolves into nothing. When it breaks, it leaves behind nothing more than a sticky mess.

The popularity religion enjoys has been purchased at a terrific price. The desire to please man has supplanted the desire to please God. "What do I get out of it?" is the approach made to this religion by popular demand. When the services are entertaining and make the participants feel good, they are stamped as successful. The world's methods and manners are religionized and brought into religion, and finances and figures have been made the test of success. A big crowd and a lot of money are interpreted as sure signs of the blessings of God, and it is considered sacrilege to question the doctrines or ethics of anyone who has been successful in gathering a large crowd and abundant cash.

In view of this seeming boom, it would be well to consider what has happened to religion. What little religion is preached is of such a shallow, frothy nature it should bring a response of disgust, but it doesn't. The strength of true religion has been so diluted it has lost its effectiveness. Cheap, sentimental appeals have been substituted for true sledge-hammer messages. What a change! What a comedown!

True religion has always offended, but today's religion prides itself in the fact it does not offend. The guilty sinner is not offended, but rather feels very comfortable with religion. Wayward Christians are not offended because in today's religion the question of sin is dealt with in such generalities, it is almost impossible to determine who is guilty. Repentance has become a forgotten doctrine confined to the yellowing pages of neglected articles of faith. What used to mean "godly sorrow" doesn't even involve mild embarrassment. The crowds have never responded very well to true repentance, so modern religion, by popular demand, has discarded it.

Contrast today's religion by popular demand with the reality of facts. Consider the moral condition of our country. The figures have been published often and do not need to be reprinted. Crime is at an all-time high. Juvenile delinquency increases every year. Divorce rates climb every year. Jailhouses, penitentiaries, and detention homes are packed to overflowing. Drunkenness and dope addiction mount with each passing day. Illegitimate births and abortions continually increase in numbers. Our headlines scream of murder, rape, suicide, and robbery. Sex-mad and whisky-soaked, the nation reels down the path of the pursuit of pleasure. The material in popular books, songs, movies, radio and television programs, et cetera, gives an idea of what appeals to America. Popular religion would have us believe we can have all this and still be religious. Who is kidding whom?

True religion will check the flood tides of sin and depravity, but this has not happened in today's religious boom. The religious boom is a spiritual bust. Religion is failing but makes a desperate attempt to appear successful. This is accomplished by using the "numbers racket." It measures everything by "how big" and "how many." Numbers have been made the criterion of success, and the church with the most statistics in its favor is judged the most favored of God. The world and religion now use the same standard of success: finance and figures. In reading the great number of church papers, bulletins, magazines, et cetera, it would be easy to conclude that religion is out to produce one thing: numbers. Church services are judged a success if there is a large crowd, and the value of an evangelistic campaign is determined by how many were persuaded to make some kind of "decision." The average church has its whole organization geared to bring about one thing: an increase in numbers and everything else is secondary.

A great number of religious papers have been reduced to nothing more than numerical reports exploiting cheap, number producing, promotional schemes. This thing has been carried so far, the average preacher feels that since numbers are the sole indication of God's blessings, numbers he must have or he has utterly failed. How many young preachers have given up in discouragement simply because they did not produce numbers? Numbers can indicate the Lord's blessings. They can also indicate many other things. Great numbers can indicate that religion has become popular by compromising the great truths of religion. Great numbers can also indicate a religion has a good program of entertainment that appeals to the non-religious.

Chapter 15
Baptized Bones

The Old Testament prophet Ezekiel was assigned a task that was most unusual. God called upon him to preach to a congregation of dead, dry bones. Most preachers have had similar experiences of preaching to this type of congregation. Ezekiel's experience, however, was unique. As he preached to the congregation of dead, dry bones, "the bones came together, bone to his bone" (Ezek. 37:7). Nearly everyone has heard the song that commemorates this event. After these "bones came together," it is said, "the sinews and the flesh came upon them, and the skin covered them above" (Ezek. 37:8). Ezekiel kept on preaching. Finally, it is said, "the breath came into them, and they lived, and stood up upon their feet, an exceedingly great army" (Ezek. 37:10). This was a real service.

Somehow, today's preachers don't seem to have the results of Ezekiel. Most of them start out the same way with a congregation of dead, dry bones. Some even get a little movement among the bones, and they might even "come together, bone to his bone" until they begin to look like something. Today's religion is content to stop about here, and this is about as far as the average preacher ever gets; the flesh and life never seem to come. Our congregations are falling short of becoming exceedingly great armies.

The Religion Racket

The result of all this is that the modern preacher and church is spending most of its time arranging dead, dry bones to look like an exceedingly great army surging with life. This is a little difficult and frustrating, to say the least, and it does present some problems. Anyone knows that dead, dry bones can't hear, yet a pastor must keep preaching and pretending someone is listening. Sunday after Sunday he delivers sermons no one seems to hear: dead, dry bones.

Dead, dry bones cannot feel; they have no sensitivity to the appeals that might be made. Today's preacher has to continually present truths for which his congregation has no appetite. The average pastor comes before his congregation with a challenging message of inspiration. He reaches the climax of enthusiasm and looks to his congregation, expecting them to be stimulated into heroic action and sacrifice. This is what he looks for, but what he sees is dead, dry bones. The Scripture says, "And, lo, they were very dry."

The pretense that a congregation of dead, dry bones is really an exceedingly great army is a little difficult to maintain. It requires a lot of doing, and a pastor really has to work at it diligently. Just about the time he gets one bundle of bones stacked up so they look pretty good, he turns around and finds that the ones he was working on the day before have fallen down, and he has to run and do a repair job. His days are consumed, running from one bundle of bones to another trying to keep the heads on, the arms in place, and the feet on the right end.

There is possibly no place where people are as sensitive and get their feelings hurt as easily as in a church congregation. A large part of a pastor's time is consumed running from one church member to another trying to soothe people whose feelings have been hurt. Someone has made a remark he didn't like, or possibly passed him by without saying, "Hello." Oh, the tragedy of it all! The pastor has to get out the oil can in an effort to get the dead, dry bones working smoothly and use a little genial glue to stick the bones back together. He generally has to hurry the job because there is always someone else who is about to come unglued and is crying for attention.

The Bible speaks of the church member "who loveth to have the preeminence." These folks must have a constant supply of recognition and praise or they'll just throw bones all over the place. Let a pastor forget to praise publicly one of these or something they do, and it will take him two weeks to get the bones back together again.

There are very few things as pathetic to watch as a pastor who must spend most of his time out calling in the homes of his delinquent church members, begging them to come to church on Sunday so he can stack their dead, dry bones in a church pew and pretend they are part of a victorious, con-quering army. With all the emphasis that is given to numbers today, the average church is so consumed with counting how many bones are present, there is no time to be concerned about the fact the bones are dead and dry.

These dead, dry bone congregations expect the pastor to be present at every social affair, afternoon tea, committee meet-ing, homecoming, et cetera. If he doesn't show up, he'll have a pile of bones that will be almost impossible to ever sort out and assemble.

The Religion Racket

The pastor finds it necessary to run a kind of complaint department. A great deal of time must be spent listening to all the gripes and complaints of the dead, dry bones. If he doesn't come up with an acceptable solution, these folks will fall apart right before his eyes. This is a horrible sight!

The preacher generally feels he must keep his ears tuned to pick up all the gossip. Few things will scatter bones like a good wind of gossip sweeping through a congregation. A preacher sometimes feels that half of his time is given in an effort to stop gossip before it starts and the other half is spent in trying to explain it away after it starts.

Another duty of the pastor is to stand guard like a vicious dog to keep other pastors from stealing his bones.

One of the really discouraging things a pastor faces is to bring in a fine, unchurched family whose spiritual interest has been kindled and then watch their expression as they look around on a congregation of dead, dry bones. Might as well try to convince them they should take up residence in the middle of a deserted graveyard.

There is nothing like a bone battle! Let a congregation of dead, dry bones choose sides and start a real church fight, and it is a sight to behold! The young pastor is usually completely unnerved at his first encounter with this kind of thing. Crushed and scattered bones are a ghastly sight. To be able to glue them back together is a rare skill.

Another difficulty that always seems to be present in these congregations of dead, dry bones is missing parts. Someone always seems to be showing up with some bones missing. One of the most common of these missing bones is the backbone. When the backbone is missing, the individual can never stand courageous and tall in an exceedingly great army but rather collapses into a puny pile of bones.

There are some who always seem to be missing the top part of their skull. This leaves them utterly devoid of any ability to think or understand. Those who continually mislay the part of the head where the ears fit can never be expected to hear, no matter how often or how loudly it might be said. Leaving the mouth part home eliminates the need for singing, praying, teaching, et cetera. Misplaced feet eliminate the necessity of marching in service. A great number find they have forgotten their hands when it comes to reaching out to drop something in the offering plate.

Mixed up bones can be a real problem. Sometimes it will be found that the same individual might have on a Baptist head, a Presbyterian body, Catholic arms, Methodist legs, et cetera. This is usually difficult to straighten out and if one is not careful, this type can wind up scattered all over town.

Another difficulty is that sometimes these different bones get out of proportion to the rest of the body. The most common of these is a mouth too big and ears too small. Always talking and never listening. Some have ears that are too big and cause them to hear every whisper of gossip in a 10-mile radius. Those who aren't missing the top part of their skull sometimes find they have one that is too small.

Maybe we need to look back to Ezekiel. In faith, he looked to God for the spiritual work that clothed the dead, dry bones in flesh and made them live. They stood up an exceedingly great army. We still have the same God. Let's turn from pretense and look for the real thing. Let's get some life in the old bones.

Chapter 16
Rejected Revelation

Despite the effort of some to promote the idea that God is dead, all of the Christian religions still accept the fact of God's existence. They may vary greatly in their concept of God, but they do agree concerning His existence. Having accepted the fact of the existence of God, it is logical to expect that God would communicate with man, and again there is a degree of unity. Nearly all of the different Christian religions accept the Bible as a written revelation from God. The Bible repeatedly makes the claim that it is "the word of the Lord," and it has to be accepted as such or be rejected as fraudulent.

The Bible presents a difficulty to most religionists. They have to find a way to accept the Bible as the word of God and yet not be bound too closely by the teachings of the Bible. To pay homage to the Bible as the word of God and at the same time ignore what it teaches requires some tricky devices.

One of the most widely used methods to accomplish the task of simultaneously accepting and ignoring the Bible is simply to keep adding to its content. Continually adding to the Bible makes it comparatively easy to keep it soft and pliable: easily interpreted to fit each generation's ideas concerning religion. Adding to the Bible is not too complicated a task. Religion just simply writes additional books; long-standing traditions can also be accepted as inspired. Finally, the accumulated additions and traditions can be interpreted to apply any way desired. The original truths are easily buried under these additions and traditions. To see how widely this method is used, one only has to look at today's elaborate religious forms, rituals, and teachings and then try to find anything similar in the Bible as it was originally given. Most of these have been added on later.

Another method used to enable one to accept the Bible while ignoring it, is to acknowledge that the Bible only contains the word of God. In reality, this means that the Bible is not to be accepted in its entirety as the word of God but that in the writings of the Bible can be found the word of God. This is very convenient. Any parts of the Bible the individual finds easy to accept can be interpreted as God's word, and the parts he does not want to obey can be rejected as not being God's word. This is widely used. Each generation, by using this method, is only bound to accept those parts of the Bible that do not interfere with their own plans and ideas concerning religion.

It may be noticed that there are a number of new translations of the Bible available. This is probably a good thing, but it also obviously has been used to an advantage by those who want a Bible but do not want to obey its teaching. Translations can easily become interpretations where original writings are re-interpreted to meet the whims of the translators. If the desire is to ignore a truth, it seems a simple thing to change its meaning in translation.

Another method is to think of the Bible only in symbolic and allegorical terms that need to be interpreted as to their real meaning. Of course, the interpretation is always one that can be fitted into the established way of life without too much inconvenience.

Christians have always expressed a willingness to attribute many things to the Jewish people. This fact is revealed in the way some Christians interpret their Bible. When they find an unwanted truth, it is cast aside by explaining that God was talking to the Jews and has no application to Gentile Christians. This enables the Gentile to accept all the easy truths and leave the difficult things for the Jewish people.

There are those in each generation who will say the Bible is to be accepted, but only to the extent that it agrees with man's reason and intellect. Anything in the Bible that does not agree with the reasoning of man is rejected.

One of the chief skills the modern minister must master is to preach the Bible in such a way that the truths that the people might find offensive are carefully confined to the eloquence of the sermon and never reach any real application to life. All this is pitiful, but worse yet is to accept the Bible as the divine, written revelation from God, and at the same time ignore it without even making any excuse.

The Bible makes hundreds of promises, instructions, and commands known in simple and concise language. Consider a few of these and compare them with the actual practice of the average churchgoer.

"Happy is he that hath the God of Jacob for his help, whose hope is in the LORD his God" (Ps. 146:5). This is a plain stated fact. Compare this description with the average, reluctant churchgoer twisting uncomfortably in spiritual

111

surroundings as he attends worship services one hour a week. The only time some churchgoers ever really look happy is when they are talking about something they did before they became churchgoers.

"I was glad when they said unto me, let us go into the house of the LORD" (Ps. 122:1). This would hardly describe the reaction a wife gets when she suggests to her husband that they should attend church. Look at the effort the church and pastor must expend to get people to appear glad in the house of the Lord when they are not!

"Serve the LORD with gladness" (Ps. 100:2). This is what the Bible says! Look at the expression on the face of Mr. Average Churchgoer when the pastor asks him to perform some service for the Lord. If this is gladness, then sadness must indeed be horrible!

The Bible says that those who trust in the Lord will be happy. They will sing and make melody in their hearts unto the Lord. They will always be glad to attend church and will serve the Lord with gladness. That not all of this is a reality is very apparent. Church members have lost their song, their gladness, and their joy. They may attend God's house but the praise is gone. They sing with their lips but not with their hearts. Service is a dull chore and it all becomes a pretense.

Consider some other things the Bible says:

"[F]or God loveth a cheerful giver" (II Cor. 9:7). The Bible teaches that those who love will also cheerfully give unto the Lord. "Cheerful giver" would seldom describe Mr. Average Churchgoer. He slips each of his children a nickel to put in the offering, while grudgingly, he drops in as much as a whole dollar and then spends the rest of the week wondering if he had been "too religious."

"Pray without ceasing" (1 Thess. 5:17). This is another direct command from the Bible, yet the average church finds it impossible even to have a prayer meeting. It is a very rare thing to find any of today's religionists giving any time to prayer.

Hundreds of plain, simple, easy-to-understand statements such as these are made in the Bible. Yet, the great majority of churchgoers simply ignore them, while at the same time, say they are God's word. If the Bible is what we say, then we are bound to accept and obey its teachings. If it is not, we ought to be honest enough to reject it and stop the pretense.

One of the most widely used passages from the Bible is called the Lord's Prayer (Matt. 6:9–13). All Christian religions make great use of this prayer, and it is universally used as a part of the worship services of the churches. The congregation generally stands and chants in unison. Let us listen.

"Our Father which art in heaven, . . ." The Bible teaches that if God is our Father we will love Him. It will be our desire to worship and serve Him. We will obey Him in the manner of children obeying their parents. We are taught that those who are in the family of God will bear a resemblance to their heavenly Father. Look at the congregation as they recite this prayer. Is this a reality with them? Are their hearts filled with love and worship? Are they obeying? Do they bear any resemblance to their Father? Or, is it mostly just a dull, humdrum of routine? A pretense?

The Religion Racket

"Hallowed be thy name." Is God's name hallowed and sacred? It must be recognized that too many can pray this prayer on Sunday morning and use God's name in vain on Monday.

"Thy kingdom come." Many of these praying "Thy kingdom come" can hardly bear to tear themselves away long enough to worship God one hour a week and then have the gall to pretend they are joyfully anticipating a time of eternal worship and praise in His kingdom.

"Thy will be done in earth, as *it is* in heaven." The Bible reveals the will of God, and yet people living in direct rebellion against this revealed will of God can pray "Thy will be done" and experience no shame.

"Give us this day our daily bread." In America, we are not giving thanks because God provides our daily bread. We are too busy filling our pocket with another product we call "bread": money.

"And forgive us our debts, ..." This phrase in the Lord's Prayer is an expression of the sinner's desire to have his sins forgiven. It involves recognition of sin and repentance. Somehow, this just doesn't seem to fit our average congregation. To be downright repentant for sins is a lost experience.

"[A]s we forgive our debtors." If God is forgiving us in the manner we forgive each other, we are in bad shape. Yet this is what we pray.

"And lead us not into temptation, ..." This does make sense. God doesn't have to lead us into temptation. That path we easily find ourselves.

"[B]ut deliver us from evil: . . ." A congregation will pray, "deliver us from evil," and then dare the pastor or anyone else to try to do it.

"For thine is the kingdom, and the power, and the glory, for ever. Amen." This wonderful expression of praise coming from our average congregation reminds one of another phrase in the Bible where Christ says, "This people . . . honoureth me with *their* lips; but their heart is far from me" (Matt. 15:8).

Chapter 17
The Missing Majority

The failure of religion today is due mainly to a neglect of the local church. For one thing, the majority of church members do not attend church. It is common for a church to have two or three times as many members as it has attendance on a Sunday morning. The popular concept of the church as a universal, invisible body composed of all those who profess religion is well liked. Most church members are like this kind of church: invisible.

The excuses that people give for not attending the services of the church are well known. Some say they do not attend because there are too many hypocrites in the church. Following this line of reasoning, the father in the home should quit his job because there are many shirkers there. The children should quit school because there are so many delinquents. The mother should stop going to the grocer because so many bad cooks are shopping there.

The wife can always excuse herself from attending because her husband won't go. The husband can decline because his wife won't attend. If they happen to be together they can blame the children: they just won't get up and go to church. If they are all present and can't blame one another, they'll reach an agreement that they don't want to leave their dog alone.

The Religion Racket

The pastor making a call in the home to urge a family to attend church is likely to hear, "Well, pastor, I know I should attend, but I don't want to make promises that I might not keep." The father knows he's going to work every morning and the children know they're going to school. The mother has club dates, committee meetings, et cetera, that she is going to make. They're sure about this, but church? Well, that's something else.

Then there is the family that never attends church but always will declare they are going to get started one of these days. If all these folks got started on the same Sunday it would look like a double Easter!

Some families, when urged to attend church, seem to take comfort in expressing their sentiment toward all churches. "I believe in all churches. They are all good," is the statement that is often heard. They believe in all churches and suppose that will excuse them from attending any!

People seem to think if they take shelter behind some difficult theological question, it excuses them from attending church. A pastor will be dealing with a man about the need of attending church and the man will reply by asking, "What is God going to do with the heathen?" The pastor could interpret this as the man's concern about his own spiritual welfare, but he knows this is not the case. If the pastor gets by this question, the next one is likely to be, "What about the 144,000?" The weary pastor thinks to himself, "I don't know, but they sure weren't in church last Sunday."

The pastor usually has answers to all these stock questions that he never uses. For instance, when someone asks,

"Where did Cain get his wife?" he could reply, "It looks like you have trouble enough with your wife without worrying about Cain's."

Some very pious looking people will always excuse themselves by saying, "I'm not going to start until I am sure I can live it." This is like a sick person saying, "I'm not going to the hospital until I get well."

When invited to attend church, some will decline by saying, "I attended church and Sunday school all my life up until a few years ago." It seems they feel they have already attended enough to last the rest of their lives. Closely related to this are those who do not attend now because their parents made them go when they were children.

A lot of folks always need Sunday to recuperate from the ailments that have plagued them all week and thus are never able to attend church. There are always those who will plead, "This is the only day I have to rest, to sleep, to play, to work at home, et cetera."

Some folks feel they are already as good as those in the church and consequently can't see any reason for attending. They would rather join the crowd outside the church than join with those in the church.

The attitude that supposedly religious folks take toward their church is a little confusing. They say everybody should attend church, yet never go themselves. They expect the church to be there when they need it, yet never support it. They encourage the effort to seek new members for a church they do not attend. Parents want their children to attend the church even though they never go.

The Religion Racket

There is the old story of the minister who had been invited into the home of one of his members for dinner. The minister looked at one of the small children in the home and asked, "What are we having for dinner?"

"Buzzard," was the reply.

"Buzzard!" the preacher exclaimed.

"Yeah! I heard Mom say we were going to have that old buzzard for dinner," the boy explained.

The attitude of children toward the church, the pastor, and religion in general is formed by what they see and hear from the parents. Generally, what they see and hear is a constant flow of belittling criticism. All this has reduced the church to the status of standing around, hat in hand, begging its members, "Please, if you get a chance and you are not doing anything else, drop in and see us next Sunday. If you can't make it then, what about the following Sunday? No? What about Easter?"

The average individual gives the invitation of the church the same response they would a door-to-door salesman who rang the doorbell while they were taking a nap.

Chapter 18
Phony Promises

Today's religion is continually making promises that it cannot keep. The tragedy is that these promises are made in the name of God, and people associate these failures with Him. Everyone has problems, difficulties, fears, et cetera, and when religion promises to eliminate all these problems, many are quick to seek this wonderful cure-all. To say that people become disappointed in their experiences with these false promises and turn away from all religion is to put it mildly.

The fierce competition for members between churches and denominations today prompts them to strive to outdo one another in making promises. Religion pretends to be a panacea that will eliminate everything undesirable and give anything that is desired.

Again, today's religion can be compared with the old time medicine man traveling around with a wagon loaded with bottles of wonderful elixir that are guaranteed to cure anything and everything. By the time people discovered it was phony, the medicine man was in the next town. The wonderful elixir generally had such a high percentage of alcohol that the user was easily deceived into thinking it worked ... for a while. Rather than admit they had been hoodwinked, many would pretend the elixir really worked. So it is with religion.

The Religion Racket

Too many are willing to pretend that the phony promises religion has made are really working rather than admit they have been hoodwinked.

The promises that today's religion are making are really something. One religious book, reprinted 16 times, has chapter headings like these:

"God Wants You to Be Prosperous"

"God Wants You to Be Successful in All You Undertake"

"Turning to God for Success and Good Fortune"—This book proposes that their idea of religion will give satisfactory answers to questions like:

"Are you in need of greater prosperity?"

"Would you like to be more beautiful and charming?"

"Would you like to own a business of your own?"

"Are you over or underweight?"

"Would you like to have more friends?"

"Would you like to have more good fortune and success in everything you try?"

"Would you like to have more pep and energy throughout the day?"

"Would you like to get married?"

"Are you unable to sleep at night sometimes?"

Now that just about covers it all. A religious cure-all. Be successful and prosperous in everything you try. Be beautiful and charming. Get a successful business. Gain weight, lose weight. Get lots of friends. Have pep and energy all day long. Get married. Sleep at night. Come one, come all: just a few more bottles left! Don't laugh. This book is in its 16th printing, and there are many more that are similar. Perhaps you bought one.

Is it any wonder when someone with a real need turns to a religion making such phony promises, that he eventually turns away from all religion in disgust?

It is an accepted biblical fact that a great deal of the physical diseases that plague us today are closely associated with our mental, emotional, and spiritual conditions. Become angry before or after eating a big meal and chances are you'll get an upset stomach. Anyone knows this, and the remedy: don't get angry. If you stop getting angry, you have a wonderful cure for stomach upset . . . sometimes. Many of our physical ailments would disappear if our spiritual conditions were healthy. To offer religion, however, as a cure-all for all diseases is downright fraudulent.

When religion gets a little more sophisticated, it doesn't offer get rich quick schemes or promise cures for lumbago, but it does put great emphasis upon such conditions as worry, anxiety, stress, guilt, fear, sorrow, et cetera. Elaborate claims are made concerning how to rid one's self of these conditions. Again, it must be stated that a great deal of worry, anxiety, guilt, et cetera, will be eliminated when the spiritual condition is healthy. However, to set down spiritual rules that one can follow to eliminate all turmoil and sorrow is to deceive deliberately. This is a fake cure-all.

The Religion Racket

These phony promises bring about another tragedy. People immediately associate the failures of these promises with the promises pertaining to eternity, and come to the conclusion that they also will fail. This destroys all faith.

Today's religion seems to have forgotten some of the basic teachings and examples of the Bible. Christ said, "In the world ye shall have tribulation" (John 16:33). It is also stated that in this life there will be tears, sorrow, and pain (Rev. 21:4). It cannot, therefore, be a sign of religious failure when these things come.

The Apostle Paul could speak of being "sorrowful, yet always rejoicing" (2 Cor. 6:10). Sorrow came, but he could rejoice in the help he received. Religion is not a cure-all for all our troubles, but it is the best source of help we have in facing these troubles and problems. The promise of religion is to provide help in facing these difficulties, not getting rid of them. Look at Christ, our example, when He said, "My soul is exceedingly sorrowful unto death" (Mark 14:34). Even in sorrow and death, God gave victory.

Today's religion has only emphasized the attractions of religion. It is not mentioned that to be truly religious means sacrifice, denial, and a willingness to live contrary to the popularly accepted standards.

These phony promises are also directed at another angle. "Successful" religious promoters will offer a set of rules for religion and guarantee success if they are followed. Seminaries indoctrinate their students with little pat schemes and ideas that are supposed to make them an instant success. One book that presents plans for making a Sunday school grow in attendance makes this statement, "No school can be a failure if it will use even one-tenth of the one thousand suggestions which are contained in this volume." In this book, failure means a lack of a great number in attendance and success means a large number in attendance. It seems such a shame that Jesus, or even Paul, didn't have this book on how to be a success.

Another book on how to be "successful" in building a large church attendance states in its introduction, "The world turns its back on a failure and listens to the man who delivers the goods and who has been successful in his field." In this book, he (the author) gives you the "how" of a successful church program. "The rest is up to you."

The world turned its back upon Christ: by this standard He was a failure. Paul, alone in a prison, deserted by his friends, and waiting to be executed, would also be classified as a failure. Again, it seems a shame they didn't have one of these books written by men who knew how to be successful.

The tragedy of this is seen in the lives of young men who give themselves in dedicated service to the Lord. These phony promises of success are held out and then they fail, too. Often a truly great life is discouraged and sometimes wasted. We need to turn from phony promises and again turn to the real thing, which is far better.

Chapter 19
A Virtue Vault

People usually prefer confining their religion within the four walls of a church building. They make a virtue vault out of their church. Religion can become an embarrassing thing to some when it gets outside of the church building. Somehow, when we take religion outside of the church building it makes us uncomfortable, even ashamed. So we normally keep it stored away in the church. It is good to know it is on deposit just in case we need it: when we die or something.

A great number of people put on religion as they do their Sunday clothes and are quick to take it off when the church services are concluded.

The religion professed is generally in such sharp contrast with the life that is lived, it seems they must be kept separate. For instance, brotherly love seems to be something entirely apart from today's fast paced, highly competitive, so-called "rat race." Brotherly love? It's dog eat dog! The unselfishness talked about on Sunday morning is replaced by the "anything for a buck" philosophy on Monday morning. "Do unto others as you would have them do unto you" is replaced by "Do others before they do you."

Truthfulness is a wonderful virtue . . . on Sunday mornings. The trouble with truthfulness is that no one believes it will work anywhere but in church. Skillful lying seems to be a necessary tool in most pursuits. Honesty is the best policy... on Sunday. Anything one can get by with is best for the rest of the week.

The Bible teaches that man is not to look on a woman to lust after her. Lusting after women is such a prominent part of life today that seemingly no one is going to allow religion to interfere. Purity, holiness, goodness, virtue, honesty, chastity—somehow, these religious characteristics just cannot be fitted into our daily living.

The task of keeping religion confined within the four walls of a church building so it will not interfere with daily living is accomplished in many different ways. The easiest way, of course, is to find a religion that is not embarrassing. The less a church believes and teaches, the less embarrassing it is in actual life. This is the type of church that doesn't make much difference one way or the other, and most folks find this convenient.

Another method used to keep religion confined to the church building is to give great emphasis to the differences in religion. This enables one to pretend to be ignoring his own religion so as not to offend someone of another religion. It can be said that religion should be kept in the church house so as not to be offensive to anyone. Even our government has made use of this method. In order not to offend anyone, all reference to religion or God must be eliminated and religion confined to the church. Using this method, it is even possible to eliminate praying from the public schools.

The word "fanatic" comes in for a lot of use. After all, one shouldn't go overboard on religion and become overzealous and enthusiastic. Everyone knows how foolish some people become over religion. This makes a good excuse for keeping one's religion stored away in church. No one wants to be a fanatic.

Of course, one can stay away from religious friends during the week and only see them on Sunday. This is a great help in keeping religion locked up in the church house.

To keep one's religion at church and not bring it into the home is a little more difficult, particularly if there are children. After all, what can a parent tell a child who begins to wonder why what he heard at church isn't practiced at home? Some parents have found that it works fairly well if what is taught at church can be associated with make-believe, fairy tales, nursery rhymes, et cetera—things that are only applicable to children. This relieves the parent from having to bring his religion home. It also enables the child to grow up without being inconvenienced too much by religion, and he can easily discard it about the same time he gives up fairy tales and nursery rhymes.

A husband and wife can usually reach a kind of standoff where neither of them expects much of the other concerning religion. It can cause all kinds of confusion if one of them decides to bring religion home from the church.

When the child starts public school he quickly discovers that religion is never mentioned. There is no particular reason given, it just isn't classified as important enough to be considered. The child at first has a little difficulty adjusting to the fact that what he learns at church might contradict what he learns and sees in school.

Folks find that about the worst thing that can happen is to discover that someone who goes to the same church works at the same place as them. This does bring about embarrassment. Every time one of them is engaged in non-religious activities, it seems as though the other is looking, and this kind of thing can lead to a complex! It almost forces both of them to bring their religion to work. Generally, though, they will reach an unspoken agreement that they will both leave their religion at church, even if they do get mildly embarrassed when they meet in a prayer meeting or some similar place.

Another convenient way of leaving religion inside the church is to develop the ability of listening without hearing. What one doesn't know about religion can't affect life outside the church house. Some have achieved a high level of efficiency at this method. They can sit down in a church pew and put on an expression of intense interest while at the same time turning off their mind or tuning in something non-religious. This is kind of a spiritual stupor. This allows them to be exposed to religion but eliminates carrying any out of the church. They've been to church in body but not in spirit. They never really know what their religion is so it never causes them any inconvenience or embarrassment outside the church. Closely related to this is the ability to pass on everything said in church to someone else and never let it be personally applied. If one can feel the religious truth didn't apply to him, he can easily leave it at church.

In our country, people move around a great deal. This affords a real opportunity for people who like to keep their religion locked up in church. For instance, a couple will get married and move away from their hometown. They have found, however, that it is convenient to keep their official church membership at the old home church, even though they do not live or attend there. This keeps their religion not only confined to a church building but also keeps it some distance away. This, they find, is an added advantage.

It seems some folks find it impossible to trust any one church with all their religion. They would rather spread it around in many different churches. They accomplish this by not being identified with any one church but make it a practice to attend many different churches. In this way, they are never associated with any one religion, and it is a comparatively easy thing not to let this kind of religion invade everyday living.

A little extreme, but used quite a bit, is the method where the individual continually finds something in church with which he disagrees, or he makes certain that he is always getting his feelings hurt. In this manner, he keeps an excuse for not attending church. The difficulty is never rated high enough to cause him to sever his relationship with the church but is always enough to keep him from attending. This enables one to have religion at the church yet not be identified with it in everyday living.

The fact that religion is continually confined to the church-house and never brought outside might be the reason it is so pale and weak. It is suffering from a lack of fresh air, sunshine, and exercise.

Chapter 20
Painless Extraction

Today's religion is often very open-minded, and just about every subject can be freely discussed from the pulpit. The preacher soon learns, however, there is one thing that must never be discussed. If the preacher does mention this subject, the faces of the men will harden; young people will become nervous and giggle, while mothers will clasp their hands over the ears of their children to keep them from hearing. One subject that is taboo: money!

In most churches, money is a dirty word. In any other area of life it is a cherished possession and is much sought after, but in church it is "filthy lucre." To talk about money seems to express a lack of faith. It just seems so non-religious. This is very strange. Nearly everyone has an income of some kind and has bills and payments that must be met. Salaries, pensions, income, bills, taxes, mortgages, prices, budgets, loans, monthly payments, et cetera, make money a very large part of daily life. Money is accepted as an honorable essential in our way of life. Everywhere, that is, except in religion.

All church members recognize that money is necessary in maintaining their buildings and activities, but no one is supposed to talk about it publicly. Preachers are among the most underpaid employees in the country. People seem to feel that since preachers are men of great faith they do not need money like anyone else. In spite of this, sometime or other, practically every preacher, directly or indirectly, will be accused of being a money-grabbing charlatan.

This attitude in the churches toward money has produced a variety of methods of getting money without really saying the word. It is a kind of painless extraction! This is a real task because everyone knows the difficulty of getting money from people without their crying out in pain. All this puts religion in an awkward position when it comes to finances. A manufacturer puts a price on his product that will cover his production costs and return a profit. The wholesaler and retailer buy the product and sell it for a profit. The employer determines what he can pay in the way of salaries, and the employee knows what he needs in wages. Theaters, movie houses, concerts, et cetera, all charge admissions that cover their costs and return a profit. This is standard procedure ... everywhere except in church.

A church will have set financial responsibilities to be met, but will have no way of determining a set income. The financial income of religion is determined by what the people happen to feel like giving. This creates a situation where the average church is always under financial stress and must wait anxiously from offering to offering to see if the generosity of the people matches the size of the current bills.

No business could operate in the manner of a church. Consider the building a church must maintain. First, there is the auditorium. In the average church of today, they are holding one service a week, which results in the auditorium being used less than two hours a week! There are large departmental assembly rooms in the Sunday school that are used about 10 to 15 minutes a week. Sunday school classrooms are actually in use about 35 minutes a week. The average large church of today must build and maintain an expensive building that is going to be used less than two hours a week! The only parts of today's church buildings that seem to get a lot of use are the kitchen, dining room, and recreation room. Today's churchgoer would rather play than pray. He prefers feasting to fasting and dancing over devotions.

In general, religion is always looking for ways of raising money. Rummage sales are a big thing. There always seems to be something a little sad about a rummage sale. There will be a little crude, homemade sign out in front of a large, ornate church proclaiming the fact that a rummage sale is in progress. Proud women in all their finery will be bringing in their old clothes to sell, and all the proceeds go to help the poor religion. Pie sales and bake sales are always popular. The generous members will each bake a cake or pie that will be sold and the money given to the church.

Pledges are a must in most churches. The pastor and a faithful committee will go around to the homes of the members soliciting a pledge for meeting the coming year's budget. Religion, the supreme possession of life, is allowed to be reduced to begging for its existence. The last thing that should ever hinder the work of religion is a lack of money. However, it usually is the number one problem. Bazaars, festivals, fish fries, car washes, bingo, raffles, paper drives, et cetera, are all used a lot by religion to raise money. It seems that the main activity of religion is raising money.

The Religion Racket

Receiving the offering is an important part of a church service. Typically, offering plates are passed among the people and they drop in their gift of whatever amount they desire. This produces some very odd situations. For instance, one member can sacrificially and regularly give a good amount every week. Another member shows up at church once or twice a year and drops in a dime, and both of these members are accepted equally in the church!

An individual who would never allow himself to be thought of as a freeloader anywhere else, doesn't seem to mind it at church. Non-supporters feel no embarrassment in knowing that there are those who are willingly sacrificing in order to maintain a church so it will be there when the non-supporter happens to attend. The non-supporter would be outraged at the idea of closing down the church he never supports. Maybe religion should be allowed to sue for non-support.

All these freeloaders and non-supporters show up on Easter Sunday and are treated as honored guests! The attendance will almost double on Easter Sunday, but the offering will stay the same!

The money given to churches is deductible when the income tax is figured. This is a big boon to churches, but it does create some problems. In order to deduct the contributions to the church, a record has to be kept of the amount given and this can be embarrassing. To give when no one knows what you are giving is one thing. To give when a record is kept is another. In order for the church to keep a record of the amount given, offering envelopes have to be used. The giver puts his offering in an envelope and marks the amount on the outside. A lot of folks have to face up to a tough decision.

First, they can suffer the embarrassment of admitting how little they are giving and use it as a deduction. Second, they can increase their giving and pretend this is what they have been giving all along. Third, they can refuse to use the envelopes rather than reveal how little they are giving. Of course, this costs them their deduction.

There is probably more grumbling and complaining about the necessity of the church continually seeking money than anything else. Listening to the average churchgoer would bring the conclusion that religion had a gun at his back and robbed him every week. Some folks complain so much about giving they don't have time to give. The church is a non-profit organization and they want to make sure that it stays that way.

Chapter 21
Emergency Religion

Although most people try to keep their religion limited to one hour a week and confined within the walls of a church building, they will all agree that it is supposed to be an ever-present part of life. It is obvious that most people do not consider religion as a constant influence, with them at all times. They would rather think of religion as a doctor, a police officer, or a lawyer. They only want it around when they feel they need it, and then they want it in a hurry.

There are times when even non-religious folks seem to want religion and want it fast. An individual who has never made any pretense of needing religion and has never attended church will suddenly want a minister to come, pray, and read the Scriptures when he gets sick. It is amazing how fast some people can get religious when they get sick, and how fast they can forget it after they recover. Nearly all sick people will promise a clergyman to be more religious and to start attending church regularly. These promises are generally kept ... at least until they are out of the hospital. If all the people in the United States would suddenly start keeping all the promises they had made to the Lord when they were sick, it would start a religious boom such as the world has never seen!

The Religion Racket

Sometimes it would seem that the only people who are religious are those who are experiencing sickness. It appears that folks are willing to give themselves to the Lord only when they are sick and cannot be used of the Lord.

The young preacher quickly learns that he must never say too much to an individual about his lack of attendance at the services of the church, but woe unto him if he is not present for a sick call every time someone's ingrown toenail acts up. It seems to be some kind of status symbol to get a preacher to call several times during one brief illness. When an individual is sick, he expects religion to come to him, but when he is healthy, he can't be bothered about going to religion.

Another strange thing is that people who never have time for religion will suddenly want it when they see their home breaking up. A man and his wife will have a big quarrel and it looks like the marriage is on the rocks so they call for the preacher and get religion. If their marriage isn't saved, they figure religion has failed. If their marriage is saved, then their problem no longer exists, and they no longer need religion.

Parents who have never bothered to take their children to Sunday school and church are quick to want help from religion when one of their sons has trouble with the law and winds up in jail. They expect religion to salvage instantly what it took them 20 years to destroy.

Hospitals have an Emergency Room, and churches should probably have a department called "Emergency Religion." The only time most folks look to religion is in an emergency.

Many prisoners in jail will make a grab at religion whenever it is offered. Generally, though, when they are released, they leave their religion behind in jail. It may as well be there as locked up in a church building. Same difference!

Religion has a responsibility to help the poor and needy and this is right and good. It is a cause for wonder, however, to observe how people who have never been religious will suddenly "get religion" when they are down and out. They will expect to receive help from a church they didn't support when they could and don't plan to support after the emergency. Missionaries on the field have found that the religion, which can give the best food, clothes, farm equipment, et cetera, will get the most converts.

Another time people want religion in a hurry is when their religious parents visit them from out of town. Folks who haven't been religious or been in church for a long time will suddenly want enough religion to last through the visit of their religious parents. They'll get up on Sunday and take their parents to church just like what they did 52 Sundays a year!

There are those who get religion every time the church gets a new pastor. Their religion wears off at about the same ratio as the newness wears off the preacher.

Some seem to think of their religion as a type of invisible inoculation against the effects of being non-religious. They seem to figure that after they are one time immunized, about one or two booster shots a year is all they need. Closely associated with these folks are those who have condensed their religion into little vitamin pills. They figure that if they pop one of these into their mouth every so often, they will never have to bother about getting a balanced religious diet through regular attendance at church.

An individual who has never made any pretense of religion in his life will have it forced upon him anyway after he dies. It is strange that an individual who was never religious and never attended church will always have relatives and friends who will arrange for a religious service at his funeral. In some instances, the only time he ever attended church is when he is carried in at his funeral and can't do anything to stop it!

Very few religious services display the sham and hypocrisy of today's religion like a funeral. The most non-religious man in town will die and then be given a religious funeral. A preacher will spend a great deal of time preparing a "few words to say" to give the impression that although the man utterly ignored all religion, he was still a good man and would be all right throughout eternity. All of the man's non-religious friends are present and they find a great comfort in this, because if their friend could live like he did and make it all right then they figure they are in pretty good shape. All religious folks present will conclude that if he made it without religion they are wasting their time being religious. Since funerals are the only religious services some people ever attend, they are really important. After going to a number of funerals and hearing everybody "preached into heaven," whether or not they were religious, it is easy to come to the conclusion that religion doesn't make much difference. And most of what is practiced today doesn't.

Another time when people ordinarily want religion is at a wedding. Folks who never attend church and make no pretense of religion wouldn't think of having their young folks married anywhere but in church. Too many times, the only time the couple ever attends the church is to be married. It is THE thing to have a big, fancy, church wedding even if one has utterly no use for religion.

People will go on year after year without ever attending a church or supporting it in any way, yet they always expect one to be there when they need to have a funeral or wedding. They surely have a lot of faith in religious folks to keep things going between weddings and funerals.

Chapter 22
Cures That Kill

It is extremely disturbing to watch as religion begins to fail. A lot of effort is always put forth to bolster a sagging religion. Many different methods have been employed to check the decline in religion. One of the most common methods used to strengthen religion is to combine it with something else. If religion won't stand by itself, join it up with another activity and this is supposed to give added strength.

Since real religion will have an effect upon every aspect of life and is closely associated with every activity, it is not too difficult to cement it to anything that is desired. Generally, it is found that such a merger has disastrous effects. Religion continues to decline and that which it has joined, rather than helping, is consuming and destroying.

The result of combining religion with entertainment has already been considered. Whenever a religion begins to appear dry, dull, and lifeless, it is logical to look around for something that will inject a little life. Too often, religion will turn to entertainment, and gospel celebrities and stars will be brought into the services. Clerical comedians will be employed. The old hymns will be thrown out and "gospel songs" with a beat will be used. The latest singing groups are asked to appear. Religious movies become a regular service rendered. At first, this combination of religion and entertainment seems to work. Generally, the crowds will pick up in attendance and folks will seem to be enjoying the services. It will appear that it is easier to get the unchurched to attend this type of church service, and usually more "decisions" will be made.

All this appears wonderful, but somewhere along the line it will be noticed that there is less and less religion and more and more entertainment until finally entertainment takes over and religion is just a faint suggestion. The church will find itself in direct competition with commercial entertainment, and in this field, the church always comes out second best. The only thing it has to offer is cheaper admission.

It has been found that to join religion with psychology and psychiatry can also be a success for a while. There can be no doubt that true religion will reach into the realms of psychology and psychiatry, but to overemphasize these in order to strengthen religion can prove fatal to religion. It is a cure that can kill.

We are living in a time of re-emphasis on things that concern the mind and spirit. The effects of emotional disturbances, nervous breakdowns, maladjustments, et cetera, are well known. The jargon of the professionals in these fields has become common to all. Books on psychiatry, psychoanalysis, mental hygiene, et cetera, are also available to everyone. Again, it needs to be stated that true religion, properly applied, is the answer to a great deal of the mental and emotional difficulties that plague this generation. It is also true that when religion over-emphasizes this, it again is in danger of losing its identity. Our church services can degenerate into mental health clinics and our preachers can become nothing more than second-rate psychiatrists. That which is an important part can be allowed to grow until it assimilates all other aspects of religion.

More and more it will be noticed that religion is being joined to politics. The close identity of these two is very evident. Preachers have found that it gets a great deal of attention to comment upon political affairs. The liberal and conservative, the right and left wing, as well as the middle of the roaders all find their political philosophies being expounded from our pulpits. Religious leaders and their denominations are looked upon as potent political factors. It is not uncommon to see conflicting sides of a political issue each being represented by religious leaders quoting Bible verses to prove their point. It is soon found that marriage to politics eventually smothers religion. Church services become nothing more than political rallies, and political indoctrination takes the place of religious teaching.

When the spirituality of a religion begins to wane, the tendency is for the adherents to feel they must get busy and do something. This results in renewed emphasis upon the various programs of the church, and the one getting the most attention is likely to be social work and welfare. The effort to secure clothes for the naked, food for the hungry, shelter for the homeless, education for the illiterate, et cetera, is intensified. Certainly all of these things are good and should be done, but if religion finds that all it is doing is providing for material needs then it is again missing its purpose. Religion will find that it is still dying...spiritually. It is again swallowed up by that which is supposed to help. The result is the same, even if a "good work" has done the consuming.

In searching about for added strength, religion sometimes joins up with recreation. A successful religion today feels it must have good recreational facilities. Some of these have reached the proportions of having fine gymnasiums, swimming pools, bowling lanes, skating rinks, et cetera, while others have to be content with a ping pong table or two. Practically every church finds it necessary to sponsor teams in all the church leagues for bowling, softball, et cetera. The church is also expected to provide for the social life of the churchgoer, and dances, card parties, and social activities of all kinds are used. This also results in failure. It causes people to attend church to play, not pray. Associating religion with recreation winds up with recreation taking over and becoming predominant while religion continues to decline.

Religion is always urged to join up with all civic improvement activities. Of course, these are important. But should it become religion's main task to improve our environment? This is another cure that kills.

The erosion and decay these things can bring about in religion is subtle and hard to define. After all, what's wrong with good, clean entertainment? With religious psychology and psychiatry? With politics? Social work? Recreation? The answer, of course, is that nothing is wrong and real religion will have an effect in all these areas. However, it is also a fact that any one of these things can dominate religion so as to destroy. We can bury religion in an overemphasis of these "good things."

It is an admission of utter failure even to feel that religion must be joined to something else in order to survive. If it continually has to be propped up, then we are in bad shape. If religion does not have strength to stand on its own, then of what possible good is it anyway? The decent thing would be to bury it quietly and try to forget it.

It seems as though very few ever think of the other alternative. Why not knock off all the barnacles that have attached themselves to religion and give it a chance? Why not quit trying to dilute it and let religion come on full strength?

Chapter 23
Sunday Sickness

It is embarrassing that the promises and precepts of today's religion are failing, and they never seem to become a reality in the life of the adherent. This situation makes it necessary for religion always to be explaining why it is failing. There are several standard excuses and explanations that are used a great deal.

One of the methods that is widely used is to add so many conditions and qualifications to the promises and precepts of religion that they become unattainable. The fact that no one can meet these conditions provides a fine explanation as to why the promises and precepts are not a reality.

For instance, religion is supposed to exercise a great deal of influence in the home, and much religious instruction is given for parents and children. Religion holds out the promise of solutions for the many problems that plague the home today. The continual rise in the number of broken homes, juvenile delinquency, divorces, et cetera, all bear witness to the fact that these promises are failing. Rather than look for the source of the failure, religion will simply keep adding conditions that give an excuse.

Religion joins with psychology and gives impossible conditions for the parent. The conditions that have to be met before the promises become a reality are almost impossible.

The Religion Racket

Don't dominate the child! Don't hold the child in check. Let the child have free expression. Don't insist upon obedience because it may cause frustrations and antagonisms against the parents.

Exercise firm discipline! The parent must teach the child a respect for authority. Don't insist upon obedience, but teach the child a respect for authority! The parent could certainly walk a fine line trying to maintain this balance.

Overprotection! The parent must never overprotect the child. This stifles the child's realization of inner security and sometimes makes it impossible to break the ties that bind him to the parent. Belonging! The child must feel he belongs. He must be protected, sheltered, and made to feel secure. The child must be protected, but not overprotected. He must feel he belongs to the family, yet be independent. He must feel secure, but not bound to the family. The parent is held responsible for maintaining this kind of balance!

Excessive manifestations of love! This is a horrible thing. Untold evil comes from this. The child will fret, cry, and be unhappy. In all his life he will never be satisfied and will only demand more and more

Lack of demonstration of love! This, too, is a horrible thing, as the child must feel he is wanted. He needs and must have love. The parent is faced with the bewildering choice: should I express my love or should I avoid such expression? How much love is excessive? When does a demonstration of love become excessive?

Rejection! This gets a lot of attention today. Every kind of wrong imaginable is blamed upon the fact the child feels rejected. The parent should never leave the child with a feeling that he is unwanted. Over-indulgence! Don't reject the child, but don't give him too many material expressions of love. Again, the parent is in a quandary trying to find the middle ground.

Excessive condemnation! Wrong should be censored but not excessively. Again, where is the line? Parents are told never to be shocked by anything that the child does. This takes some real doing!

The child's feelings are to be respected. Fear and punishment are to be avoided. Parents should be consistent. Parents should never make the child feel inferior. Parents should never force the child beyond his capacity. Parents should answer the questions of the child but never beyond the child's understanding. Parents should show interest in the child's activities. Parents should never expect perfection. Parents are not to be antagonistic, dominating, or over-identify themselves with the child. And, on and on it goes!

About the time a parent has finished wading through all these conditions of being a success as a parent, he accepts being a failure, spanks the child, and forgets all about it.

Another method used by religion to excuse itself for failure is to blame someone else. Pass the buck! It is very convenient to blame the non-religious for all the failures of the religious. Our morals are at a new low, crime is increasing, juvenile delinquency is out of hand, lust rages, sex is distorted, and drunkenness is a national scandal. All these are evidences of the failure of religion but are accused of being the cause. This is like blaming pain as the cause of the injury.

The Religion Racket

Of course, each religion can always blame another religion for the failure. This is done a lot. The pastors can always blame the people and, in turn, the people can always blame the pastor.

One of the really surprising things is that weather has so much effect on religion. A lack of attendance at church is always listed as one of the reasons for religious failure. A great percentage of folks will not attend church when it is raining or snowing, or when it is hot or cold. In the southwestern part of Ohio, it is estimated that it will rain about 10 Sundays a year, snow on at least three, and it figures to be hot 12 Sundays and cold for at least nine. This makes 34 Sundays these folks cannot attend church. They will have company visiting their home on about eight Sundays and will be away visiting for about another eight. This makes 50 Sundays a year these folks cannot attend church. It leaves two Sundays a year they do attend: Easter and Christmas . . . if it doesn't rain or snow!

Sunday sickness is given as another contributing factor to the failure of religion. Many folks are very fortunate since sickness never seems to come on a weekday when it could cost them money by losing work. It never comes at a time when they have planned some pleasurable event. Always on a Sunday! Then they can just lie around in bed and sort of enjoy being sick.

A lack of money is always listed high among the excuses for the failure of religion. No doubt, this is a real problem, but one cannot help but wonder how much money it takes to make the love, peace, joy, assurance, et cetera, of religion a reality in life? How many more expensive church buildings will have to be built before America becomes religious?

Some of the excuses that religion gives are a little contradicting. Some are saying that if we could just get back to the good old days, everything would be all right. The "old time religion" is the answer. Others tell us religion is failing because it is dragging behind the times. It needs to be modernized. That is the answer.

Brainwashing is sometimes used to cover up religious failure. Brainwashing is the procedure whereby an individual is convinced that what he has always believed to be the truth is a lie and what he has always believed to be a lie is the truth. The individual is exposed to a constant repetition of a lie told as the truth and a truth told as a lie until it is accepted as such. Brainwashing has been going on a long time in the name of religion. The general attitude of the public toward religion has been molded by this procedure. Some lies have been repeated long enough and loud enough so that just about everyone accepts them as truth. Religion itself has been guilty of propagating some of these lies and some have been imposed upon religion by outsiders. As has been noted, this brainwashing can reverse the meaning of religious words and terms. Right becomes wrong and evil becomes good. In order to cover up its failure, religion simply brainwashes people into thinking failure is success and success is failure.

Many times, lies that are accepted as truth are presented in little standard clichés with which everyone is familiar. To suggest that these much-used expressions are not true is to evoke the wrath of those that are using them as a shield, but it still needs to be done. Most people are familiar with these clichés.

"You do not have to attend church to be religious. You can be just as religious outside of the church as you can in the church." This has been said often enough and loud enough so that most people accept it as the truth without giving it any thought. One little question exposes this lie. If this statement is true, why was the church established? Using this line of reasoning, the church becomes excess baggage and should be discarded, and yet people who use this expression would probably be the first to protest if this were proposed. Religious truths have been preserved through the church, and yet religious folks can adopt the lie that the church isn't needed.

"It doesn't make any difference which church you attend. One religion is as good as another." This statement is widely accepted. It seems such a good, loving, tolerant attitude to take. As has been stated, all religions are obligated to accept what they believe and teach to be truth. Too many times the "truth" of one church contradicts the "truth" of another church; in fact, everything that any church believes is denied by another. To look at all these contradicting creeds and say it doesn't make any difference is to reveal how successful this brainwashing has been. Creeds that contradict cannot all be true. Some have to be in error. To say there is no difference is to eliminate the distinction between truth and error! This is foolishness.

"There are so many different religions it is impossible to know which is right." This lie is readily accepted as the truth because it seems such a good excuse for rejecting all religion. Are we to assume that the God of religion was not able to preserve the truth and make it available to all? Has God been defeated and His truth hidden? No! The very fact that we have a God assures that we have His truth and the responsibility of recognizing and believing that truth.

"The Bible is so complicated that no one can really understand it." Too many people have been turned from the Bible because they were brainwashed into accepting this lie as truth. This statement can also be shot down with one question: If the Bible cannot be understood, why was it given? The very fact that we have the Bible establishes that it was to be understood and believed. What purpose would God have in confusing or in keeping us in the dark?

"The Bible doesn't really mean what it says." People find a comfort in this lie because they can write off anything in the Bible they do not like. If the Bible doesn't mean what it says, then why did it say it? Why didn't it say what it meant?

"It is best to allow a child to pick his own religion without any influence from the parents. It is best not to force the child to go to church and Sunday school." No one would use this kind of reasoning anywhere else but in religion. Do we allow the child to decide whether he should go to school? To the dentist? To the doctor? Do we allow him to pick his own medicines? If it would be foolish to allow these things, then it would be doubly so to apply the same reasoning to matters of religion.

"Too much religion can drive you crazy." "Too much religion" would be a condition so rare in America as to be almost non-existent. Trying to maintain the pretense we disguise as religion can endanger our sanity.

The Religion Racket

"You can't be religious and happy at the same time." The caricature of the churchgoer as a miserable, straight-laced sourpuss has been well established. People have been brainwashed into thinking that being religious and being unhappy are synonymous.

What is really needed is a willingness to turn from our excuses and find the source of the failure of religion.

Chapter 24
Female Trouble-Shooters

The Bible has much to say, and many illustrations are given, establishing that the responsibility of leadership in religious matters was given to the man. Adam, the man, was created first and Eve, the woman, was to be his helper. The responsibility of leadership continued in their sons, not their daughters. Those who were saved from the flood were led by a man, Noah. Abraham and all the patriarchs were men, as were Moses, Joshua, and all 13 of the judges that ruled Israel. All the kings and all the prophets were men. The old priesthood of Israel was composed of men. The 12 apostles and the early church leaders, preachers, deacons, elders, evangelists, missionaries, et cetera, were all men. The woman is spoken of as "the weaker vessel" (1 Peter 3:7), and "the head of the woman is the man" (1 Cor. 11:3).

All religion knows that this is taught both in instruction and by example. To say that the woman has never been satisfied with this arrangement is to put it mildly. To say that the man has always willingly accepted this responsibility is to be ignorant of the facts.

In the beginning, religion was going good in the Garden of Eden until Eve decided to take over and Adam consented.

The Religion Racket

When Eve, the woman, took over the leadership in religion, all chaos resulted that has lasted until today.

One of the biggest of the shams of today's religion is that which presents man as being in the position of leadership in religion. Religion knows that man should be leading, so it pretends he is even when they know it is not a reality. It is obvious to anyone who cares to observe that women dominate religion while still feigning submission to the man.

More women attend church than men. A large percentage of the men who do attend are generally there because their wives insisted. More women teach Sunday school classes. The spiritual leader in the average religious home is the mother. Ordinarily, there are more women's organizations in the church than men's, and more women hold church offices. More women than men generally sing in the choir. It is a fact that the influence of the woman dominates the average church and the average religion. Most of the established religions have begun to ordain women and to use them as pastors, evangelists, missionaries, et cetera. A large percentage of the more recent religions were started by women.

It has to be said that in most instances men have willingly relinquished the responsibility of leadership. Sometimes they have submitted only after a long battle. The lack of men has created a void in religion that women have tried to fill. That this is a fact is one thing, but to pretend that it is not is another. For women to dominate religion while keeping man as a mere figurehead is rank hypocrisy. It so cheapens and belittles man as to create a response of disgust.

Too often, a man's name is listed as Pastor and he stands in the pulpit, but in reality, the church is "pastored" by his wife. He is a mere figurehead, a stooge. This kind of pastor preaches the sermons that his wife has deliberately influenced and in some cases designed. She uses him to pour out her vengeance upon any who dare question her leadership. She uses the influence of the pulpit as a weapon in all the feuds and church fights in which she cares to participate. By her interpretation, to disagree with her is to disagree with the church. To displease her is to set oneself up as the target for next Sunday's sermon.

The pastor's wife generally shares the same kind of intimate knowledge concerning the personal affairs of the membership as her husband. If she so desires, this knowledge can become a deadly weapon used to keep the membership in submission to her rule. This type of pastor's wife pictures herself as a "church queen" and expects everyone to pay homage at her throne.

Sometimes it seems the pastor's wife must assume this dominating role to provide some self-protection. She finds that this must be done or else she must stay hidden out somewhere most of the time. No one can be the "target for today" as much as the pastor's wife. Everything she does is subject to the closest scrutiny by the other women of the church. They delight in "picking her bones," and it is always open season. How she dresses, keeps house, raises children, works in the church, et cetera, are all examined continually under the magnifying glass, and discussed freely by all.

This kind of condition where a man is a mere figurehead is also a reality in many of the other positions of leadership in the church. The man holds the office, but the wife manipulates the strings and he responds as an obedient puppet.

One of the arts in which a pastor must develop a great deal of skill is keeping peace with all the different women's organizations in his church. Too many times a pastor has had to retreat from the field, battered and defeated, after making the mistake of incurring the wrath of an organization of women. One thing these organizations will not tolerate is for a mere man, even a pastor, to try to give them any leadership. A pastor, like all other men, finds it difficult to understand women. A women's organization can be nailing his hide to the wall, ruining his ministry, and sending him to his study battered and beaten, while at the same time they are baking his favorite cake and taking up money to buy a new suit for his birthday!

The Bible presents a contrasting picture of a woman. She is used as the symbol of the highest form of holiness, the bride of Christ (Ephesians 5), and also as a symbol of the lowest in depravity, the harlot of the 17th chapter of Revelation. She is pictured as contentious (Prov. 27:15), subtle, and deceitful (Prov. 6:24). Yet her love is the finest of all virtues of mankind (1 Sam. 1:26). She has brought about the greatest good and yet is responsible for the greatest harm. These characteristics of the woman show up in each generation.

Most churches will periodically find themselves wracked with divisions that can degenerate into real church fights. These do irreparable harm to the cause of religion. One thing these church fights and divisions all seem to have in common is that they are started by women.

Most women religious leaders fall into one of several categories. There is, of course, the crusader. Her type is probably the best known. She is always riding at the head of a righteous cause ready to do battle with any and all who stand in the way. The crusader always thinks of herself as the defender of the faith who is going to right every wrong. She charges from one committee meeting to the next, whipping in line the less zealous.

There are the female religious leaders who are the reformers. Generally, they are women who never enjoyed sin very much themselves, and they are going to see that no one else does.

Some of these women religious leaders could only be tailed losers, as nothing they ever do succeeds. They hold regular committee meetings where they carefully plan each defeat. Their whole assumption is that religion doesn't have a chance, so they make a career of rejoicing in defeat.

Then there are the sufferers. These are the female religious leaders who are always loudly proclaiming how silently they suffer for the cause of religion. These women are generally planning to suffer anyhow, and they figure religion gives them a reason. Most people can't stand to see someone suffer so these women wield a powerful influence.

Another group might be called the organizers. Their main characteristic is being busy, busy, busy. They are the "take charge girls." They always move with great speed and efficiency in getting every religious project organized, complete with all details. They also generally wind up being "Madam President."

The Religion Racket

Trouble-shooter is a position that many women religious leaders covet. A trouble-shooter is one who feels that it is her job to take the leadership in helping those in trouble. Let a man and his wife have a fight and the trouble-shooter is right there to help them patch it up. Helping young girls in "trouble" is a specialty. Advice on rearing children is freely given. Helping a wife with a wayward husband is a delight to the trouble-shooter. One of the added advantages of being a trouble-shooter and possibly the reason it is so sought after is that it enables the trouble-shooters to get all the latest gossip first hand. This really makes them the hub of activity.

Women have been successful in keeping men who are religious leaders in submission by a method known as "hero worship." It is really very simple. Women will look upon a man in a position of leadership as a white knight and will give him all the accolades and plaudits that are his due as a hero. No mere man can resist this and will do anything to maintain his "hero" status, even to the submitting to every whim of the women.

Religion got into trouble in the beginning when Eve decided she was going to take charge and run things her way. This difficulty reoccurs every time this attempt has been repeated. Yet it must be said that if it had not been for faithful women, religion would have gone out of business a long time ago. The blame for women dominating religion has to rest with the man. It is because of his failure that this condition exists.

Religion needs men who will drop the pretense and in reality give the spiritual leadership that is needed in the home and in the church.

Chapter 25
Point of No Return

A merica is like a man with a fear of cancer who will not go to a doctor because his fears might be realized. We run faster and faster and never stop to look at ourselves. Maybe it will go away, but we know it won't. The sickness gnaws away and the fear persists but we keep turning from the truth. We try to bury this gnawing fear under the tinsel of prosperity and pleasure, but it doesn't work. It has become a way of life to ignore the warning signs. We know the diagnosis, but we won't accept it. We even know the remedy but won't use it.

We must stop and look at ourselves. Not in the light of our own publicity and not in the light of what we'd like to think we are, but we need to look at ourselves as we are in reality. Listen to the first chapter of Romans (vs. 21–31):

"[W]hen they knew God, they glorified *him* not as God, . . ." The pages of history are cluttered with the wreckage of nations who followed the same downward spiral that characterizes America today. Our only distinction is that we are doing it faster. No nation can survive which, after knowing God and His blessing, rejects Him, and this is the course that America has taken. A nation, which, in the very beginning, was characterized by an acknowledgment of its need of God and His blessings, now is engaged in systematically eliminating God from every aspect of its existence.

"... but became vain in their imaginations, ..." Somewhere along the line, this country began to feel it no longer needed God. Instead of acknowledging that our greatness was in Him, we began taking the credit. Our accomplishments were our own doing. We were the greatest. God? Who needs Him?

"Professing themselves to be wise, they became fools, ..." Religion followed the trend. Man-made religions that exalted man rather than God multiplied rapidly. Man was safe in the shelter of his own intellect.

Religion was constantly changed to meet the current whims of the people.

"Wherefore God also gave them up to uncleanness through the lusts of their own hearts, to dishonour their own bodies between themselves: ..." When a nation rejects God, decay and degeneration begin. The slide into the abyss of moral perversion accelerates fast.

"Who changed the truth of God into a lie, ..." In this path of decline, the nation eventually finds that it has completely changed directions. We made a 180-degree turn. Black is now white, error is truth, chaos is order, wrong is right, et cetera. On and on toward complete degeneration, the point of no return! We need to stop long enough to look at ourselves.

"... vile affections: for even their women did change the natural use into that which is against nature: ..." We have degraded our women from the exalted place of respect and beauty to a brazen, naked symbol of sexual depravity whispering out invitations from every billboard, magazine, movie, play, book, et cetera.

"…men…burned in their lust one toward another;…" Men lust after men and women after women in a full expression of vile affection, and we are told by some religions this is as it should be! We listen as pasty-faced reprobates speak of a "new morality" in which sexual depravity is declared the accepted thing. The sickening thing is that we listen.

"Being filled with all unrighteousness, fornication, wickedness, covetousness, maliciousness; full of envy, murder, debate, deceit, malignity; whisperers, Backbiters, haters of God, despiteful, proud, boasters, inventors of evil things, disobedient to parents, Without understanding, covenantbreakers, without natural affection, implacable, unmerciful:" Our children are in ever increasing numbers turning to crime. Mobs roam the streets bent on violence. Lying, cursing, and bitterness are the order of the day. Destruction, misery, and bloodshed are our daily diet, and we do not know the way of peace because we have forgotten God.

We know, even when we won't face it, that our nation today is saturated with unrighteousness, fornication, wickedness, covetousness, maliciousness, envy, murder, pride, and boasting. Have we passed the point of no return? No nation that has ever gone as far down as we are has ever come back. It can, but it never has been done. There is absolutely no hope, unless we are willing to look honestly at ourselves and admit what we are. America is sick, terribly sick, but we won't accept the diagnosis or the remedy.

The Religion Racket

In the face of this sickening mess, religion busies itself with building bigger and better hospitals that the sick will not attend, and arguing over the ingredients of medicines that no one will take. When someone does come for help, religion responds by covering over the cancer with empty platitudes and hollow pretense and blandly announces that everything is going to be just fine. A lot of religion spends its time trying to convince dying patients that they are not really sick!

This nation has a malignancy and religion hands them a patented happiness pill. Well, maybe we'll die laughing anyhow!

EPILOGUE

This book began with the statement that "religion in the United States is a failure." Each chapter has emphasized some aspect of that failure.

Real religion is buried under a maze of contradicting claims, tired traditions, and the deliberate deceits of our religion racket. We have constantly practiced pretense in religion so long that it has become a way of life: habitual hypocrisy.

Religion is supposed to be characterized by brotherly love, but in reality, the average church is a place of fretful feuding and frequent fighting. Most of today's churches were started by groups that got licked in a church fight and had to move out.

In general, religion has become a highly competitive business with hallelujah hucksters peddling packaged piety and bargain blessings. This competition and proselyting brings a response of disgust, and it should.

Instead of dedicated worship and sacrificial service, today's religion is offering what might be called ecclesiastical entertainment. This association of religious truth with mere entertainment has so cheapened the truth that no one takes it any more seriously than they do the patter of a nightclub comic.

Religion has made itself look ridiculous by making the preposterous claim that all the hundreds of competing churches with their bigoted beliefs, contradicting claims, and diverse doctrines are really one religion.

It is an obvious fact that the high ideals, lofty goals, and high-sounding phrases of religion do not find much expression in daily life. The sham and hypocrisy of modem day religion is brought into glaring light when we compare what we are with what we profess to believe.

The antics of the "spoiled saint" are well known and bring reproach on the name of religion.

The feebleness of the church's effort to teach religion has produced a generation of spiritual ignoramuses. Man's effort to produce a "do-it-yourself" religion has proven to be disastrous.

The continual diminishing of the amount of time religious folks give to religion is a real indicator of the unhealthy condition of religion. Churchgoers trying to be religious and sinful at the same time are a pathetic sight. Professing belief in the Bible while at the same time ignoring it is ridiculous.

Today's religion keeps making promises it cannot keep, and the world looks upon it as a failure.

Religious folks keep their religion locked up inside a church building and then wonder why it has no effect on the outside world.

America is like a man with a dread of cancer who will not go to a doctor because he is afraid that his fears will be realized. Maybe we have passed the point of no return.

In every aspect of life where religion is supposed to wield an influence, it is falling. This sums up the diagnosis that has been made.

Is there a remedy? This is the question that naturally is asked. There is a remedy, but it is so simple that our sophisticated age will scoff. Our wisdom makes us too proud to listen. It must be remembered that our sophistication, pride, and wisdom have produced many religions...religions that are failing.

This generation likes to think of itself as having grown beyond the need of anything as simple as the remedy that the Bible offers, but it is the only one that has ever worked or that ever will work. Let us not stumble at its simplicity.

First, there has to be recognition of the fact that something is wrong. As long as we go on keeping up a pretense of well-being and refuse to acknowledge our need, there is no hope. In all honesty, we need to look at ourselves as we are and acknowledge the desperate spiritual need that we have. If religion is failing, let's admit it. If we have a hunger for something real in religion, let's look for that which will satisfy and bring assurance.

We have to come to an understanding of our responsibility in this failure. Anyone who honestly looks at his spiritual condition today must feel a sense of shame. We like to kid ourselves into thinking how good we are when inside we know better. We would rather bury our shame and sorrow under pretense, but we need to recognize that it is the honest, healthy thing to feel sorrow and shame for our miserable spiritual condition.

The Religion Racket

When we finally recognize our condition and become ashamed and disgusted, it is a comparatively easy thing to be willing to reject it: to desire to turn from it to something better.

Does all this sound familiar? There is a word the Bible uses to describe what we are saying. One word: "Repent!" This is a word that is used over 100 times in the Bible. Every nation that has followed the path that America is now traveling has heard the same: "Repent!"

The Scriptures record that "Jesus began to preach and to say, Repent" (Matt. 4:17). The Scriptures also reveal that God "commandeth all men every where to repent" (Acts 17:30). This is the remedy. God has made it simple and man has tried to make it complicated. Are we willing to listen?

We have listened to our man-made religions too long. We need to acknowledge they haven't worked. The Bible puts it this way: "It is better to trust in the LORD than to put confidence in man" (Ps. 118:8). It also says, "Trust in the LORD with all thine heart; and lean not unto thine understanding" (Prov. 3:5). Trust in the Lord! This is so simple we can pass it right by in more frantic efforts at religion. It seems we can't believe that anything that simple can be the solution. Yet it is!

Trust in the Lord! Is this too difficult? We should find it easy to believe, to put our faith in Him. Again, the Scripture tells us, "That your faith should not stand in the wisdom of men, but in the power of God" (I Cor. 2:5).

Repentance and faith produces a reality in our religion that makes sham and pretense unnecessary. It is all summed up in one sublime statement that Jesus made: "[R]epent ye, and believe the gospel" (Mark 1:15). Repent and believe!

We need to return to reality in religion.

A reality in assurance: "He that believeth on the Son hath everlasting life" (John 3:36).

A reality in peace: "Peace I leave with you, my peace I give unto you" (John 14:27).

A reality in love: "And the Lord make you to increase and abound in love one toward another" (1 Thess. 3:12).

A reality in happiness: "Happy is that people ... whose God is the LORD" (Ps. 144:15).

A reality in worship: "Serve the LORD with gladness: come before his presence with singing" (Ps. 100:2).

A reality in life: "[T]he fruit of the Spirit is love, joy, peace, longsuffering, gentleness, goodness, faith, Meekness, temperance" (Gal. 5:22–23).

The Bible contains hundreds of these promises. They are for real! They work! They produce a reality in religion. They are an anchor, sure and steadfast. This is the remedy. It is the only way. We need to throw out the substitute and again demand the real thing.